AD ACADEMY EDITIONS

TOYO ITO

Architectural Monographs No 41

ACKNOWLEDGEMENTS

Front Cover: Tower of Winds, Yokohama; *Frontispiece:* House in Magomezawa, Chiba.

All visual material and text is courtesy of the architect unless otherwise stated. Photographic credits: Driade, p39 (below right); Naoya Hatakeyama, pp6, 86, 88 (both images), 89, 96, 98 (all images), 108; Meyer und Kunz Fotografie, pp70 (below, l to r), 71; Jan Münchenberg, p70 (above); Tomio Ohashi, pp2, 10, 14, 27 (below centre), 34 (above left, below left and right), 36, 39 (above left and right, below left), 40-1, 42, 45, 46, 48, 50, 56, 58, 61 (all images), 63 (all images), 64, 67 (all images), 68, 72 (both images), 74 (both images), 77, 78, 80, 81, 82, 84 (all images), 85 (all images), 90, 92 (all images), 93 (all images), 94-5 (all images), 104, 105 (below left and right), 106 (both images), 118 (Kenchikubunka 1995.6), 121 (all images, Kenchikubunka 1995.6), 125 (all images), 126 (all images); Shigeru Ohno, pp52, 54-5 (all images); Shinkenchiku, pp32, 34 (above right), 51 (all images), 100 (both images), 102-3, 105 (below centre), 110 (below), 113, 114, 117 (all images), 124; Koji Taki, pp26, 27 (below left); Hiroaki Tanaka, pp27 (below right, *Japan Architect*), 30 (above right); Shuji Yamada, p28

Architectural Monographs No 41

First published in Great Britain in 1995 by
ACADEMY EDITIONS
An imprint of

ACADEMY GROUP LTD
42 Leinster Gardens London W2 3AN
Member of the VCH Publishing Group

ISBN 1 85490 270 9

Distributed to the trade in the United States of America by
ST MARTIN'S PRESS
175 Fifth Avenue, New York, NY 10010

Printed and bound in Singapore

CONTENTS

ARCHITECTURE IN A SIMULATED CITY

Toyo Ito

Aerial photographs of Tokyo are projected on the floor. One scene is flat and homogeneous, taken from three hundred metres above and graphically processed by computer. Another shows, from behind, a row of young boys playing game machines. The view then abruptly changes to a scene on an expressway as if taken from a video game. This disappears into the depth of the screen with the speed of Akira on his motorcycle. By graphic processing, the screen is flattened, completely without depth and now all we see are dramatic cartoons.

Opaque acrylic panels pave a floating floor ten metres wide and twenty-eight metres long. A translucent five-metre acrylic screen undulates along its length, incorporating a liquid crystal screen which can be electronically controlled in transparency. Another side wall is finished with aluminium panels, and a translucent cloth hangs from the ceiling. All these screens receive images from forty-four projectors, eighteen of which are suspended from the ceiling and project images on the floor, while the remaining twenty-six project overlapped images from behind cloth screens.

Numerous images edited and stored on twelve laser discs display everyday scenes in Tokyo: flocks of people on zebra crossings, businessmen talking on the platform while waiting for a train, a young man speaking on a public telephone for example. These video images are collaged and incessantly changed on the forty-four screens, which reiterate and fracture the sequences of images by turns. 'Environmental' music processed by a synthesizer fills the space from sixteen-channel speakers to add a further dimension.

This is the exhibition 'Dreams' in the third room of the 'Visions of Japan' show held in London. Visitors are showered by floating video images and soaked by sounds. Their bodies float on the river of the acrylic floor and sway as if they were seasick. The Crown Prince of Japan opened the show and said he wished he'd had a cup or two of sake before he came so that he could experience the show more vividly. Prince Charles on the other hand, asked me what could possibly follow these images. When I answered there might be nothing to follow them, he asked if I was an optimist. I said of course I was one.

'Dreams', according to its producer Arata Isozaki, was originally titled 'Simulation' since it presents a simulacrum of the present-day Tokyo. The title was revised in response to those who believed that 'Simulation' was too difficult for the general public to understand. Tokyo *is* a simulated city in a sense – the experience of viewing these images is almost like walking through Kabukicho Street at night. We are exposed to tremendous video images and showered with sounds. By looking into the screen of the video game, we see ourselves already within it. We are both intoxicated by the illusion of light and sound as suggested by the Japanese Crown Prince, and suspended in a futureless void as implied by Prince Charles. Perhaps there is no future to reach.

There exists, however, a distinct difference between the simulation in the room and the reality in Kabukicho. While the real town is endlessly filled with noise and chaos, the collage of a city displayed on-screen can soon be filled with white noise or phased out into the stream of computer graphics. In short, the urbane scene will lose its definition and fade into morning mist. All the realistic scenes melt into a state of calm enlightenment – a kind of 'nirvana'. If we are to imagine the future, what states other than extreme technological control can we expect?

Five objects appeared in the shower of video images in 'Dreams'. Designed by the young Englishman Anthony Dunne, these looked like TV sets fresh out of their packages or comical androids breathing the information-filled air. They converted images in response to noises or generated strange sounds. Commercial TV sets are ready-packaged just as businessmen don suits to unilaterally convey mainstream information. These objects are highly personal and poetic, and allow us to rediscover that we are surrounded by noises. We may yet have acquired an additional organ within the body which can inhale noises like objects. Our bodies are constantly yet imperceptibly exposed to the air of technology; we respond to it, and synchronize our biological rhythm with it. Unconsciously, we may already be developing a robotised existence.

The Okawabata River City 21 Town Gate B, known as the Egg of Winds, was based on a similar concept. An egg sixteen metres long and eight metres in diameter was wrapped with aluminium panels and now floats in front of two high-rise apartment buildings. The egg is merely an object which reflects the sunlight in daytime but at night, by means of five liquid crystal projectors, it displays video images, both recorded and live, on the internal screens and on the perforated aluminium-panelled surface. The silver, shining egg possesses at night a vague three-dimensional existence without the reality of even a hologram. Passers-by look up at the egg, stop for a moment to wonder what it is, and then walk away. The object differs from the street-post TV sets or the large Jumbo-tron colour displays which decorate the walls of buildings downtown. It receives video images which can be seen through the information-filled air which encloses it. This is the object of images which comes and goes with the wind.

Coinciding with the creation of the Egg of Winds, a similar model was displayed in a Brussels exhibition. This was the initial model of the River City 21 Town Gate B, shaped like a ship or a polyhedron with trianglular planes. The egg in Brussels was constructed from transparent acrylic material on the floor and covered by translucent cloth and perforated aluminium panels. Visitors cannot enter it but can see chairs and tables installed inside, through the translucent covers by natural light from above. They see city life packaged within the egg just like an illusion. They are all transient objects; like a mirage, without the feeling of texture or existence. They are ephemeral objects, more akin to spontaneous phenomena like rainbows than to structures. Originally intended as the model for a future house, the Egg of Winds was too costly to develop, but it fulfilled my aim of enabling people to see a new lifestyle in a simulated city, through the medium of air.

If we think of the two 'egg of winds' together, we may perhaps call them the 'design of winds'. We should be able to use a 'filter' to view information contained in the air, so that we may visualise it. Architectural development should lead towards the discovery of such a filter.

The Tower of Winds which I built a few years ago in front of Yokohama Station in Japan embodied most efficiently the design of the winds. The tower is characterised through its installation amidst the neon-lit downtown rather than in a museum. Although the tower winks in a less spectacular fashion than the other neon advertisements, it is said to give the impression that the air around it is filtered and purified. This may be so, since my intention was not to cause a substance to emit light into the air but to convert the air itself into light.

The Egg of Winds in Brussels was created for the exhibition 'Pao: a Dwelling for Tokyo Nomad Women', and for me, was a model city house. It depicted the image of urban life which daily loses reality in proportion to the visualisation of that life. The two eggs therefore share a common feature: they are both containers implying new life. I wanted to show that the loss of reality in city life is the 'flip-side' to image-like architecture.

In any age, a dream for a new life leads into a new space. In the mid-seventies people dreamed of a modern way of life in a home filled with electric appliances. It was symbolised by a open, flat-roofed or brightly-lit house covered by a small gradient roof; a kitchen with a built-in refrigerator and a gas oven, dining chairs with chrome-plated pipe frames and thin bentwood backs. A nuclear family was comforted by such bright images of modernised life. A father in a white shirt worked in a modern office, constructed with steel and glass, and came home to such a kitchen and dining room where his smiling wife and children waited for him. If a Volkswagen or a Citroën 2CV was parked outside, the image of new life would have been perfect.

While ideal life in the electric age was essentially embodied in modern living, we have not yet found a suitable location for ideal life in the computer age. Instead it is more effectively reflected in the difference between the Volkswagen or Citroën of old and the Toyota and Nissan of today, rather than in houses. More precisely, Volkswagen and Citroën were designed to imply a variety of mechanical functions, while today's Japanese cars, incorporating various electronic gadgets, are submerged beneath superficial package designs that do not hint at the diverse technology inside. Today's cars are designed as if the image is now irrelevant to the mechanism, a concept becoming more and more applicable to other household purchases.

While car and industrial design pursue a modern style to fulfil the fashionable requirements of consumers, house design is entirely orientated towards conservatism, even though it too is superficial. In the world of architecture where function and form were never closely related to each other from the beginning, style was directed to the nostalgic expression as Japan's gross national product increased.

What then, is the new life of today? We are too busy to give serious thought to this question as a plethora of small fashionable items catch our eyes. Food, clothes and daily necessities on the shelves of department and convenience stores shine brightly as if in answer to our dreams. But when we have eaten, worn or installed them in our homes, they lose their brightness and fade. From that moment, we are doomed to look again for items to replace them.

A constant process of homogenisation lies behind the shaping of these products, which look superficially quite individualistic, ranging from groceries to houses. As observed in the car design of today, homogenised contents permit trivial differences in the superficial character. Architecture is destined to develop in the same direction, for example, the progress in air-conditioning severs a building from the local climate and proves that houses of any style can be built anywhere in the world. Works of architecture which are apparently unique are homogeneous in content as they are only superficially decorated with different forms. They are not unlike a fillet of fish: a perishable, wrapped in a sheet of 'Saran-wrap' on a shelf of a convenience store. Only when so wrapped and frozen under uniform conditions can they be displayed.

Since the birth of steel and glass, we have long sought 'universal space'. However, universal space which almost corresponds to the coordinates of Euclidean geometry, did not quite achieve homogeneity even though it is theoretically homogeneous. The trend towards a purely uniform neutrality was checked by local variation and the desire for monumentality in architecture. Its thorough homogenisation has been prevented by an almost unconscious worship of 'architecture' by architects themselves.

In today's architecture the phenomenon of homogenisation is expressed quite differently from the aesthetic pursuit of universal space. What is homogenised today is society itself, and architects are vainly fighting against it. The more an architect relies on characteristic or personal expression, the more homogeneous become his works as if points on the coordinates of Euclidean geometry are similarly connected. Now is the time when all society is being 'shrink-wrapped' and hermetically sealed.

Once architects longed for homogeneity because society then was in a state of confusion. They tried to incorporate transparent and neutral grids into society, which was opaque and heterogeneous as lava. But even if they had successfully attained homogenisation in a universal office space it was limited within an enclosed territory, and if they stepped outside the office it was into a real and muddy space.

Today our environment is filled with vacant brightness. Just like commodities filling up the shelves of convenience stores, our cities have dried up and become bleak. For the last ten years, they have been removed of humidity as if thrown into a gigantic dryer. Although we are surrounded by a variety of goods, we are living in a thoroughly homogeneous atmosphere. Our affluence is supported only by the thin film which keeps the cities together.

Simulated life is a construction based on this film which covers society. It has invaded offices and houses instead of remaining in a neutral zone such as downtown. Before going home after work, people stop at places in order to eat, sing, dance, talk, watch movies, go to theatres, play games or go shopping. The time and space between office and home is fully fictional. They eat whatever is served as if the dishes were home-cooked, sing and dance as if they were movie stars, discuss topics with somebody as if they were the best of friends, go shopping to perpetuate fantasies of wealth, and exercise at a sports club as if they were running in a field or swimming in the sea. Even our family life is now simulated: we can no longer distinguish reality from unreality.

We have not only lost the visual sense in terms of reality, but also taste, hearing and touch. We are no longer sure what is delicious, or whether what we hear and feel is true. Our bodies have changed even though we are not aware of it. This is because goods and communication systems have undergone radical changes: we have transformed ourselves so that we could reverse the poles of reality and unreality by the simple manipulation of an image.

The progress of media has resulted in the isolation of words from products, diluting the reality of the products themselves. We have developed images completely unconnected to any physical reality. The simulated life has proliferated into other areas to the extent that unreal communication has become so necessary in our daily lives that other forms of communication are impossible. Communication which was once deeply rooted in an area or local community has lost its significance. The thriving element in our cities is a network of instantaneous, ephemeral, and unspecific but numerous media which deny physical distance.

There are two challenges when building architecture in a simulated city. One is how to create a work of architecture with a physical presence that goods no longer possess. The other is to build architecture which endures while local communities are nullified, and the forms of communication mutate incessantly. Such contradictory problems are difficult to solve, but what kind of architecture is possible without their resolution?

There appears to be no definite solution, but what is certain to me, however, is that it is meaningless for us to stand to one side ignoring these problems. We must strive to resolve the contradictions. Firstly, we must learn to make fictional or video-image-like architecture: and secondly, we need to make that architecture ephemeral and temporary. I do not mean that architecture should be replaced with video images or that temporary buildings should be used. We should rather build fictional and ephemeral architecture as a permanent entity.

We should utilise the power we obtain from these cities in order to create space, and should fully use the effect of their fiction. From impulses gathered in the cities themselves, I have suggested fictional and ephemeral images by utilising light and video images for the Tower of Winds and the Egg of Winds. I have attempted to evoke naturally occurring fictional and ephemeral images by using liquid crystal glass screens in several projects: the Japanese Maison de la Culture in Paris, the Nakameguro T Building, and the F Building in Minami Aoyama – the latter two utilised stripes created by pasted silkscreen films. I have also tried to create images which were more natural than nature by building artificial landscapes on originally flat sites, in projects such as the Guest House for Sapporo Breweries, and Gallery 8 in Yatsushiro.

These manipulations are all simulations – there is no architecture which is *not* simulated in these unreal cities. The hill in front of Gallery 8 is quite artificial, but once completed, seemed to have been there for over a hundred years. Reality today is created beyond such fictionalism. We are now living in the borderless world of reality/unreality, and this is reflected in our architecture. When all society is pre-packaged and hermetically sealed, all we can do is beautifully visualise the wrapping rather than attempt to make the content look real. How we define the structure of this fiction will determine the fate of architecture.

PAGE 6: 'Visions of Japan' exhibition

TOYO ITO: STEALTH FIGHTER FOR A RICHER POST-MODERNISM

Charles Jencks

'I want to design architecture like an unstable flowing body.'
Toyo Ito, RIBA, 1993

There is a paradox about contemporary architecture during the interregnum between ruling paradigms. Architects, like politicians, adopt ambiguous positions to attract free-floating adherents from a variegated audience, the rainbow coalitions which form and break up over single issues. Some architects take on the protective colouration of Modernists, black and white suits of respectability; others adopt the mix and match informality of the young professional; others still are tieless, or aggressively styleless. Architecture in an era of uncertain culture cannot afford too much conviction or self-assertion, which is why some architects, such as Peter Eisenman, have begun to extol the virtues of 'weak form'. Others still hide behind a supposed functionalism, a degree-zero aesthetic or Minimalism.

Toyo Ito, usually dressed in black and white and conveying his architecture between silver covers of an understated monograph, is often mistaken as the quintessential Modern architect of the moment. His lightweight steel structures and perforated aluminium surfaces place him, for the unwary, in the high-tech or Late Modern tradition. His diagonal planes and flying vaults seem to confirm this reading, as much as for the fact that he studied under the Metabolist architect Kiyonori Kikutake. Kenneth Frampton likes to portray him as one of his long-suffering existential heroes, 'symbolising the void' with his harsh metallic structures, denying himself the pleasures of heavyweight building like some ascetic monk lost in the silence of 'spiritual stoicism' and empty forms.[1] Given the laughing Buddha smile that momentarily breaks across his face, this won't do. Other critics, because of certain influences, have compared him to Rem Koolhaas, or because of his temperament and background have slotted him in the 'Shinohara School' – those architects such as Itsuko Hasegawa, who have been influenced by Kazuo Shinohara and have a formal commitment to the Silver Aesthetic.

None of this pigeon-holing seems very relevant, at least to Ito's personality and work as a whole. These escape classification, slide beyond the categories. I have a theory, which may not be invariably true but seems mostly right: the better the architect, the more unclassifiable he or she is, the more different facets the work reveals on investigation. If each individual has multiple selves which they develop – parent self, consumer self, ideal self, tentative self, as social psychologists label these constructs – then any good architect exploits this psychological kaleidoscope. Behind the consistent facade of silver grey, Ito's work shimmers with heterogeneity.

Ito the Traditionalist

In his talk at the RIBA in the summer of 1993, Ito presented his work obliquely as typically Japanese, alluding to its equivalences with Noh Theatre (where masks are put on and meaning is implied rather than stated), and its relation to Zen (where buildings, like his Tower of Winds, are meant to heighten the senses). With this building the sense of sound and the sense of wind – actual events on the street – are recorded and immediately played back graphically on the facade. An interactive architecture reflecting moods of an evanescent and abstract kind is the equivalent of a Zen landscape painting featuring mists, mountains and wind.

Very often Ito mentioned the floating nature of his architecture, a clear allusion to what is called 'The Floating World' of Ukiyo (Ukiyo-e means 'floating world pictures', especially the wood-block prints which depict everyday life). Uki can mean 'transient', 'impermanent', and therefore sad and evanescent, or 'lively', 'gay', and therefore dynamic and urbane. With his view of the typical nomad woman of today, flitting from stage to stage in the daily theatre of Tokyo life (a character to whom Ito often alludes and often designs for), it is clear he intends both ends of this spectrum. He is not censorious, nor romantic, about this new urban character, but sees his architecture depicting and furthering her life, a gentle background for life in the 'Simulated City', as several of his projects are known.

Ito the Techno-Futurist

The idea of the contemporary city, particularly Tokyo, as an evanescent theatre of signs and symbols, the play of information across facades and the changing skin of the environment, started in the 1960s with the rise of semiotics. The architect Minoru Takeyama was the first to apply this emergent science to the urban scene, then Roland Barthes wrote his *Empire of Signs* in 1970, and by 1977 Ito himself started to represent this aspect of city life: his PMT building, which became well known in the West, stretched out a strange modulating aluminium skin. This 'unfunctional' extravagance was meant to proclaim its independence from interior requirements, and thereby represent the grey 'superficiality' of consumer society. To Westerners it might just look like a sensuous version of Richard Meier's world built in silver slick-tech, but for Ito it was more a suitable background for life in the information society. If this life is always changing, always a simulation of something else and if there is no correspondence between exterior wrapping and interior function – a consequence of electronic simulation – then the designer must propose a suitable response. 'I do not mean,' he writes in *Architecture in a Simulated City* (1992) 'that architecture should be replaced with video images or that temporary buildings should be used. We should rather build fictional and ephemeral architecture as a permanent entity.' In other words the fictional signs the architect creates – images of nature, undulating hills, wind, mist, forest, and things that change in everyday life – should be enduring. Representing change in permanent form was a goal of both the Futurists in 1915 and the Metabolists in 1960.

Since the PMT building he has produced a number of such background/information-foreground structures, most notably the Tower of Winds, and the 'rotating oval' for the Japanese Alphaville, known ominously as 'Okawabata River City 21 Town Gate B'. During the day the rotating oval looks very much like a hostile intruder, perhaps an aluminium boat or blimp tethered awkwardly between two ugly tower blocks. But at night, when the commuters pour home from work, the aluminium skin dissolves and through its perforations the scurrying thousands are entertained by images projected on liquid crystals: not one story or set of images but a computer-scrambled assemblage of five different image sources. This 'Egg of Winds' simulates the rush and colourful twinkle of an information society speeding every which way.

The most convincing version of the Simulated City was constructed for a short time at the Victoria and Albert Museum, in the exhibit 'Visions of Japan'. This was assembled and directed by the architect Arata Isozaki (whose grey aluminium 'twilight architecture' has certain affinities with Ito's). Here Ito created, with the help of eighteen projectors, acrylic floors and walls of liquid crystal, an extraordinary illusion of a simulated city – a double simulacrum – where images and noises went through all four planes of the room and the observer felt he had intruded accidentally inside someone else's brain to float around between firing neurons and exploding holograms. The effect was mesmerising, hypnotic, disorientating, intoxicating. When I visited the exhibition, on more than one occasion I found spectators lost in a trance: indeed once I found the old-time Archigrammer, Ron Herron, sitting cross-legged on the floor soaking in this electronic nirvana, trying to fathom its secrets for his own liquid crystal buildings.

For Ito there is a kind of nullity or nihilism inherent in the meaningless succession of frenetic images that shoot across this electronic landscape – a 'white noise' that characterises the information age, a noise full of every sound but without melody, theme or significance. Coming from an Eastern culture he feels this nullity itself can be deep with meaning; certainly with aesthetic potential. So it is turned into a sublime dreamscape, the equivalent of Freud's oceanic experience. But here cars, neon and moving crowds take the place of the ocean. Again the 'floating world' becomes the operative metaphor as he describes the installation, '... clouds or mist ... the luminous floor is a light controllable floating floor. The image slowly flows on its resinous surface as if it were floating on still water and the substances seem to melt and disappear'.[2]

We are here back in the electronic nirvana of the Futurist Medardo Rosso, who insists on the transience of appearances. Underneath it all, Rosso insists, 'we are all of us merely lighting effects' – that is what x-rays and quantum physics tell us we are. This 'backwards Futurism', the metaphysics of 1910, reveals a lot about the strengths and weaknesses of the contemporary avant-garde (and in this case Ito *is* part of a recognisable group or pigeon-hole). On the one hand the advance guard today tends to sacrifice plot for information; narrative and quality for a huge quantity of random imagery – it does not understand that the basic truth of the information age is not the quantity of data but its significance, its meaning and how it coheres together in a story. On the other hand, Ito's Simulated City certainly does convey the aesthetic equivalent of the consumer society, and it turns the unpromising world of hype and movement into a new ecstatic experience. He, perhaps more than any other architect, has captured the poetry of our electronic wasteland – so a formal inventiveness, as displayed in the Victoria and Albert exhibit, redeems a conceptual poverty.

Ito the Poet

Behind all the high-tech, hard-edged materialism, behind the cold steel and grey concrete which colour everything in the twilight of an advanced industrial wasteland, is a personality that does not mind declaring itself poetic. The disarming, indeed charming aspect of Ito is his humorous light touch, his modest irony. One might overlook Ito in a crowd of big-name architects; certainly he disappeared into the background of individualists and superstars when I saw him in Nara in May 1992: Jean Nouvel, with his brand image of black on black and rolled up jacket-sleeves; Jim Stirling and Richard Rogers, with their dayglo shirts and aggressively casual appearance; Charles Correa, the personification of the Holy Man and Hindu Sage. A hundred such individualists all asserting their special genius made Ito's quiet, understated, black and white presence all the more interesting, if one could perceive it. I'm not sure this modesty is altogether a virtue; after all, Kisho Kurokawa laments the conformity inherent in a consensual culture: 'The Japanese bang in the nail that sticks out'.

Nevertheless, Ito's light touch and restraint have power in a profession given to heaviness and the macho personality. This airy quality is most evident in his 'nomadic' furniture: thin structures, balloon shapes, tent-like struts that easily lift off the ground and disappear. Behind his floating world is the deep metaphor of the tent. Sometimes it becomes explicit, as in the Silver Hut, the house he built for his family between 1982-4. Here he imagines himself the archetypal nomad in the urban desert, living off a second or third nature of discarded domes, paper-thin building elements and anything to hand. He is the 'ad hocist', the handyman, the *bricoleur*, the savvy consumer, assembling his 'primitive hut' from the silver cast-offs of an over-productive society. The idea of cobbling together one's classical hut from geodesic domes and used car panels has been around – and in practice – since the Hippy domes of Drop City in the 1960s. But none of these examples, to which Ito alludes, reaches the aesthetic and conceptual sophistication of his home. Structured on the module of the Tatami mat, divided by thin walls that could be shoji screens, this set of parallel vaults also alludes to the classical temple and the work of Louis Khan – all of that while still being a modest lightweight structure. What sets the

Silver Hut and the Silver Aesthetic of Ito apart from Western work in the same genre is this poetic allusiveness. Like Fumihiko Maki, Ito takes advantage of the small power tool revolution to bring handicraft and individual choice to the building site. Admittedly, this is only possible within a Japanese building context, which is not, as it is in the West, cramped by legislation and legal documents. One can still make creative decisions with high-tech materials at the last moment, and hence the whole industrial aesthetic has a poetic dimension, a flexibility and an ease of the spontaneous gesture, which is lost in the West.

Ito the Post-Modernist

The historic and poetic allusions which are definitely present are also definitely displaced into a new code. Ito says of the lightweight screens in his house: 'They are like shoji, but if I use paper it's too classic'. The allusion must be transformed; tradition must be acknowledged *and* displaced at the same time. An understated double-coding – and its overstated variety is the hallmark of American Post-Modernism – is evident everywhere. This double-meaning pulls together different eras and opposing discourses; it cuts across the usual boundaries of audience and carries on the Post-Modern agenda – the binding of time and disparate audience – in a new way.

Because Ito is a Post-Modernist dressed as a Modernist, his message has an unlikely freshness that takes one by surprise. Can he really see high-tech steel as the flexible equivalent of paper or wood – or even the spontaneous brushstroke of the Zen ink painting? What does he mean by the title of his RIBA talk 'Architecture as Garden: Garden of light, Garden of mind, Garden of microchip'? What is this deep metaphor of garden, coding the non-natural to the organic?

Ito's commitment to underlying metaphor, and 'green architecture', mark him as the quintessential Post-Modernist. The materials and imagery he uses would put him outside the accepted tradition of the Greens – after all, aluminium is one of the most energy-expensive materials available. But his thin structures always sit very lightly on the earth, and often burrow one or two storeys underneath it, connecting architecture to the landscape, saving energy with earth berms and understating the impact of the man-made.

The small museum in the Kumamoto Prefecture is a case in point. Old trees on the site were carefully preserved as the billowing steel vaults bent this way and that around them. The museum was itself conceived as an artificial park, digging below ground and thereby pushing up a green mound of earth near the entrance. Over this gentle grass slope (a 'fictional or simulated hill') stretches a flat bridge, a gently curved arc only three inches deep, that hovers just one or two feet over the earth – like a bow stretched taut.

Everything is done to increase the lightness of the building, its floating quality; the very antithesis of contemporary museums in the West. Where our collections are housed in mausolea and temples, as if art consisted of relics to be hoarded and worshipped, Ito places artefacts under tent-like shapes behind glass and perforated metal and – most unusually – locates the storage space in a huge, hovering cylinder. This, the flying wedge of Zaha Hadid, or the extruded egg of Will Alsop, or the flying beam of Kazuo Shinohara, may be the fashionable shape that these precedents suggest, but it is also an ingenious solution to keeping works of art. Usually this storage space is put out of sight, underground, a subconscious not accessible to the public. But, again a usage from the past, storing artefacts in the air as in the old Japanese Shoso-in, is transformed in the present, but without explicit reference. It is the double-coding of an underground Post-Modernist working away by stealth, disguising the many layers of reference behind an industrial vernacular.

In such work, Ito positions his architecture at the juncture between traditional Japan and the computer age, and reveals the eternal hidden in the ephemeral. Such antitheses and double-coding challenge us to look again at the customary way we classify architects, and question the categories of architectural production. If metallic building can be as delicate, humorous and flexible as this, the twenty-first century can rewrite the doleful history of machine age architecture which has bored and imprisoned us by turns.

Notes

1 Kenneth Frampton, 'Ukiuo-e and the Art of Toyo Ito', *Space Design*, 86:09, pp144-7.
2 Toyo Ito, 'Space/Simulation/Visions of Japan', 1991.

PAGE 10: Yatsushiro Municipal Museum

TOYO ITO: THE LIGHTNESS OF FLOATING

Irmtraud Schaarschmidt-Richter

The general perception of Japanese architecture is still influenced by the classical clarity of the imperial Katsura Villa, dating from the seventeenth century – a building that was greatly praised by both Bruno Taut and Walter Gropius and that has greatly influenced modern Western architecture. However, little consideration was given to the fact that there had already been highly complex building with abundant, imaginative decorative elements[1] in Japan, if one did not look for the 'exotic' side of Japanese culture. Traditionally in Japan, architecture is regarded as belonging more to technology rather than to art. Only a few architects or builders from ancient times are known: famous carvers of building ornaments or Kobori Enshu (1579-1647), who has entered Japanese cultural history but as an expert on gardens and a 'tea-master'.

Modern Japanese architecture, however, soon had an important position in world architecture (which it retains and develops today) having taken the first steps in the twenties and thirties and creating its own form of Modernism following World War II. Contemporary Japanese architecture is highly imaginative. Although banks rarely finance unusual buildings, and official buildings tend to be conservative, numerous 'rather strange'[2] buildings were constructed in Japan that have brought their architects world-wide recognition. They not only appear 'strange' but also show forceful articulation and demonstrate a new construction method beyond any conventional form, while not uprooting themselves from their cultural heritage. Names such as Kunio Mayekawa, Junzo Sakakura and Kenzo Tange have long since been accepted by the international architectural world, as well as many from the subsequent generation: Fumihiko Maki, Arata Isozaki, Tadao Ando and many more.

The Search for a New Perspective in the Electronic Age

More than half a generation later, Toyo Ito has become part of this group although he is not actually a follower. He seeks a new perspective from his own point of view and development. Considering the progression of time and social changes, Ito realises that a new form of architectural thinking is needed. He does not, however, lose sight of his roots: he does not superficially take over traditional Japanese forms such as the tatami mats and the modulor[3] resulting from the average distances between supports, but his buildings and theories display an affinity with the construction traditions of his country. That means his highly specific relationship to nature and time creates a particularly Japanese atmosphere, yet Ito is completely devoted to the present. While

taking modern society into consideration – high-tech society, media information and consumer problems – Ito does not believe that an architect is responsible for this. He does, however, acknowledge that he cannot separate himself from it,[4] but confronts it, accepts it and searches for a modern means of working with it.

The world of the microchip is both a symbol and a concrete challenge for Ito. All that applies to mechanical objects, the relationship between form and function, no longer applies here. The form of an automobile, for example, is influenced by the necessity of having the least possible air resistance – such relationships, however, do not exist between the function of an electronic object and its form. The enormous capacity of a computer to store or add vast amounts of information does not necessarily lead to formal articulation. We cannot imagine the flow of electronic information, says Ito, we see only the data feeding the computer and the results it produces. Yet 'one does imagine microchips in a certain manner . . . this is linked less to form than to a space through which invisible objects are flowing',[5] spurred on by electronically packaged information.

An ever-changing flux is implied in this imagined space, full of constantly flowing matter. Ito regards it as a never-ending flowing; a flowing of people, cars, winds, plants, topography and the sounds between buildings. 'I believe that an architect should implant a type of filter, in order to make these various streams visible'[6] – architecture as medium. In his essay, *Architecture in a Simulated City*, he says we should 'build fictional and ephemeral architecture as a permanent entity'[7]. He suggests using fleeting forms such as light or video for this purpose, as with the Tower of Winds or the Egg of Winds. He tries to create scenes that flow easily into one another as in the cinema. These scenes are therefore characterised by regular change and are fictions created by technology. He does not, however, wish to replace architecture with video. Instead he wishes to reach beyond the conditions of modern society, which he describes and recognises as consumer society, pass beyond this fiction while at the same time acknowledging it. He remains uninterested by any ideological concept: thus his work is not intended for spaces controlled by computers that exclude people to a large extent.

Although Ito has designed a large number of office blocks and other buildings with comparable requirements, his fundamental experiences are based on residential buildings. His interest in the city is directed less towards urban structure than to the way city dwellers live. Apart from this marked subjectivity, he tries to understand the mechanisms developing behind modern society[8] in order to concentrate on the position of the individual. One gains the impression that despite the great freedom of his designs, he places man himself at the centre. The metaphoric description of what architecture should be is also expressed thus: 'architecture is reduced to something that protects the human body as comfortably as possible, as comfortably as clothes.'[9] – what are the mental and physical steps Ito makes in order to attain this goal?

Participant or Opponent – Experiencing Nature in East and West

Ito's working methods and expressive means can only be understood by considering the fundamental differences between Western and Asiatic attitudes toward nature. While the West regards man as being in opposition to nature, trying to bring it under control and make it useful, the Orient still sees itself as part of nature (but not necessarily subordinate to it). If one considers classical Chinese or Japanese landscape painting, in particular those created in monochrome ink, this is more easily understood. The human figure, in the form of a traveller, fisherman or simply in a meditational pose, is painted in the same brush strokes as trees, rocks and mountains. The figure is seen on a natural scale, often in the middle or even in the background of the painting. Several landscape elements offer the viewer a 'doorway' in the foreground, so that he can enter it himself, follow its course with his eyes and blend in with the whole. In Western painting until Modernism on the other hand, human figures usually appeared in the foreground, or at least in the middle – set up as if on a stage. Landscape appears more or less as background, or as an environment only in its relation to man: man stands in opposition to nature. This is still the case with Romantic paintings such as those by Caspar David Friedrich.

These differences between East and West can also be detected in the attitudes toward architecture and construction. The traditional Japanese house is a wooden framework construction whose light walls have been mere 'hangings' of no bearing function for hundreds of years. One can usually remove the sliding doors and thus change the space or push the outer walls aside completely so that light and wind pass through the building uninterruptedly and both house and inhabitant can communicate with the natural surroundings. Conversely, classical Western architecture confronts nature with its fixed brickwork: attempts to exclude it as much as possible even though devices such as window-walls that can be fully opened are found in modern architecture – influenced by Japanese architecture. Naturally, one must also consider climatic differences, as well as the change in building methods even in Japan, initially as a result of Western influences and subsequently due to modern developments. It is therefore necessary to find a new approach to nature, more abstracted and pragmatic, within a modern society (as is possible only in Oriental culture), ruled by information technology, consumerism and dominated by the media. This means emulating nature through work by empathising with it in a highly concrete manner – by becoming part of it. This still happens repeatedly in the present: a sculptor such as Isamu Wakabayashi[10] reflects this with his iron sculpture 'Valleys' and his garden designs – the sculpture becomes landscape, the landscape sculpture.

Poet of Winds – Poet of Light

Before turning to landscape and including the earth and ground in his ideas, Ito regarded the elements of air, wind and light as essential for his definition of space. Some have called him a 'poet of winds', although 'poet of light' is just as applicable. In one of his early works, the residential building White U (1976), he created a brilliant play of light. The white concrete building, consisting of two parallel U-shaped walls, and a roof pitched inward, receives daylight through a large door which opens towards the inner courtyard and most efficiently through several skylights. A performance of lights on the white walls, reminiscent of an abstract sculpture with its curves, fractures and edges, reveals the successive phases of the day. Spotlights installed in the floor echo this, leading to a dialogue or interactive game between technology and nature. Ito himself describes the White U as a 'garden of lights'. This particular kind of lighting led to the creation of 'a space that flows and fluctuates.'[11] Similar effects were repeated in the design of the House in Kasama (1989), although this has numerous exterior windows.

The ITM Building, an office building in Matsuyama on Shikoku (1993), is a very different garden of lights. Light is not directed in a particular manner with the use of skylights and side lighting, but the whole building appears like a sculpture of light that can certainly be described as a garden in the sense of Japanese landscape sculpture. Daylight enters from all sides and fills the building, a large glass wall extends over the three storeys, linked only by light, structurally indispensable columns. The glass is covered completely with foil in order to limit the impact of ultraviolet rays. Very soft light, rather reminiscent of the diffused light created by the paper-covered shoji windows of classical Japanese architecture, is thus created. All materials used in the building – glass, aluminium and white tiles – reflect light, so that one gains the impression of weightlessness.

Ito by no means rejects computer technology, he uses it to create his plays of light. Even here, a certain link to nature is maintained, even activated, as Ito makes use of the force of nature and assigns it certain functions. This started in 1986 with the Tower of Winds at the JR Railway Station in Yokohama. During the day a shimmering aluminium tower rises from a small topiary garden hiding an uninteresting ventilation tower; a structure that has no real architectural function and is largely hollow, as is known from pagoda architecture. Acrylic mirror panels cover the ventilation tower. The outside is surrounded by an oval cylinder of perforated aluminium plates. One thousand, two hundred and eighty miniature lamps were installed between the two layers, as well as twelve white neon rings and thirty floodlights, controlled from inside and outside by computers. One can easily discern the construction by daylight but at twilight the lights are switched on and a game commences – the mirrors reflect the lamp light which shines through the perforations, rising up and down in a rhythmically glittering fashion like swarms of stars moving through the cosmos. The neon rings answer to the changing light of the surroundings, while the floodlights change their intensity and the strength of their rays according to the direction and swiftness of the winds. The miniature lamps react to sounds and vary their rhythm accordingly. The flow of air, wind, sounds and changing light are transformed into electronically produced illuminations. Invisible nature is visibly transformed into aesthetic information by modern technology creating a constantly fluctuating event touched with the melancholy of passing beauty. The object Ito calls the Egg of Winds, created with similar ideas in mind, appears even more palpable. This enormous egg-shape on stilts, sixteen metres high and eight metres wide, with ends like the nose of a jet plane or the Shinkansen locomotive is actually an access to a car park, serving as a landmark at the entrance to a huge block of flats in Tokyo. Encased in two hundred and forty-eight aluminium panels, of which sixty are perforated, it shimmers in silver during the day, rather like the Yokohama Tower. In a similar way, the Egg of Winds comes to life only when daylight fades, to greet and surprise homecomers. The liquid crystal projectors within the Egg project images, videos and TV programmes onto the inner screens and the partially perforated panels which penetrate the outside. Computer-control-led images appear with the alienated quality of a hologram, a plastic object made of light which makes the quantities of air-held information transparently visible. As Ito says, these images come and go with the winds.

Ito installed another similar project with purely technical methods — in 1991-92 he took part in the exhibition 'Visions of Japan' at London's Victoria and Albert Museum using 'space simulation'. This was a video installation with images from Tokyo projected onto curved walls and reaching across the floor in constantly changing sequences, mingled with voices and sounds until suddenly everything dissolved into the sea of the 'Planet Solaris'. A soft white space was thus created where all objects appear to melt into one another and disappear. Although this is pure technology, a certain relationship with nature is retained (even if it is largely man-made) through the use of city subjects and the Planet Solaris. Such projects, however, can only be realised in exhibitions.

One Only Sees the Present — Utopias in the World of 'Nomads'

The term 'wind' which Ito uses for his first two projects is more than simply a metaphor. Objects are the tangible expressions of the elusive aspect of nature surrounding mankind; its invisible force. This has become the starting point for Ito's architecture: a new concept of architectural thinking (although it has always been present in Japanese ideas about architecture). It is, above all, an expression of transience closely related to the manner in which one perceives the present moment. Ito once stated: 'I only believe in the pleasure of the moment,'[12] — he is certainly not referring to banal amusements but to that singular moment which can be grasped only by the mind and in which past and future are one and the same, as in the 'eternal now' formulated by Kitaro Nishida, whose philosophy considers the 'past and future wiped out by the present.'[13]

This philosophy indicates constant transformation, since a moment can never be static. Classical Japanese architecture expresses this highly accurately: just as space can be quickly altered by removing dividing walls, only a small amount of permanent furniture limits a room to a specific function. In palace architecture a thousand years ago, movable silk curtain stands were used to separate oneself from others and to change position frequently. It is here that the roots of a deeper understanding of tradition can be found. Ito also realises that the future exists solely in the present. These insights into the ever-changing nature of things, in which nature itself plays a large part, and relating this to Post-modern information-controlled society, allow Ito to see the present situation of man in the urban context as a 'world of nomads', dominated by constant change and the temporary.

Therefore he believes that architectural space actually begins with the red and white pieces of cloth which the Japanese use to form a place set aside for festive gatherings. A passing event such as a tea party[14] is simply indicated by a red carpet — a provisory stage set for man, its purpose aimed directly at the person.

What could come closer to this than imagining the tent as the basic structure of a new manner of conceiving architecture? Ito lent 'concrete' architectural form to the tent in the Pastina Restaurant (1989) — a steel frame construction, combined with a roof consisting of triangular panels, hanging from steel ropes and jutting out widely, light as a tent, almost floating. The small building has three storeys, one of them underground. A steel stairway leads to the restaurant on the upper floor, made of narrow, elegantly curved tubes that emphasise the impression of lightness and floating. The diffused light, created by opaque and transparent glass walls, gives the appearance that one is sitting in an airy white tent. To Western eyes this construction already appears to break with the traditional building concept of 'space surrounded by walls'.

On the basis of that experience, Ito searched for his own, new architectural language: 'a temporary circus tent, as transient as a rainbow.'[15] As early as 1985 and again in 1989, he brought his ideas to their most extreme form of fruition with his mongol tents Pao I and Pao II. These are habitations, or better, simply temporary stations that can be thrown together and transported. Both Pao projects were dedicated to the 'nomad women'[16] of Tokyo, whose home is actually the entire city and who need only a place to sleep, eat, read, telephone and privately recuperate somewhat in order to appear once again on the 'city stage' to which they belong.

Pao I has the floor plan of a circular tent, similar to an igloo. It is made of a light, steel frame, covered by partially perforated metal plates, so that one can distinguish furniture from outside — some made from textiles in the shape of a fish-trap. The tent still stands on the ground, even though it is flexible and can be easily moved by runners in the manner of the silk curtains in the palace halls a thousand years ago. Pao II on the other hand, is a ship of winds utterly exposed to the surrounding elements and can be imagined floating over the city, 'swimming above the Tokyo sky like a weightless spaceship'.[17] The polyhedron of triangles has a transparent acrylic floor, while the walls consist of translucent material and perforated panels. Natural light entering from above streams through it. Everything appears transparent, even the furniture. It is an ephemeral construction that seems as if it would float away at any moment, Ito also calls this construction Egg of Winds, relating it to the filter that makes information contained in the air visible. Both objects were constructed solely for exhibitions in Tokyo and Brussels[18] and must remain utopian. Pao II, the Brussels Egg of Winds, became the prototype for the Egg of Winds above the car park entrance in Tokyo.

Ito has moved on from these utopian projects: in 1986 he developed the Nomad Restaurant from the idea of structuring wind and hovering on it. This is a light and transient structure that seems to sail on the winds. The carrying element is a light steel frame like those used for ordinary tents. It has been adapted to the plot of land and shifted asymmetrically, with an extension and an intermediate storey. There are no fixed ceilings or walls, instead, numerous panels made of stretched metal and perforated aluminium float above the heads of the guests, over and alongside each other, curved like the wings of large birds or sails. The balustrades are covered by cloth – an illusion not unlike a *fata Morgana*. It appears as if it could disappear into the air at any moment. The restaurant no longer exists: it was a temporary building, conceived simply as a transitory moment in time.

Ito had similar construction ideas for a temporary Noh theatre at the Tokyo harbour. He again used steel bent to form a frame, floating panels that look like sails made of expanded metal and cloth, covering the entire complex. This was another very light and abstract building, highly appropriate for the sublime, abstract art of Noh theatre. It is interesting to note that there was already a temporary Noh theatre in Tokyo one hundred and fifty years ago. The idea is therefore not so new, although Ito's project gives a much clearer expression to the transitory nature of the structure.

In 1988, Ito developed his ideas further and created the fascinating project, Playground Twelve Metres Above Ground, that could also be described as a hanging garden above Tokyo – exposed to the winds, light and nature over the roofs of the great city. Once again created for an exhibition,[19] Ito widened several roof areas for this purpose, added greenery here and there, placed small, open buildings, spanned tents and umbrellas over large areas and linked everything with hovering planes or bridges. He thus created a fascinating, communicative landscape over the roofs and streets of the pulsating city glowing with lights. Ito envisages placing small schools, theatres, sports clubs and cafes there, twelve metres above the ground, and having markets, parties and exhibitions here. He says that 'this is my great dream'.[20] It is still utopian – a dream idea, a momentary game.

Ito's Beginnings – Searching for Reality in Urban Life

Ito's biography and the list of his architectural works makes it more than clear that he is not simply playing games or dreaming. He achieved a great deal architecturally in the years after the opening of his first office in 1971 and took up various teaching posts at home and abroad. He was born in Seoul in 1941, and graduated in architecture from Tokyo University at the age of twenty-four, joining Kiyonori Kikutake's office in 1965. The latter was one of the co-founders of the Metabolist Group[21] whose main aim was to find a synthesis between public and private space, leading to the extreme nature of their constructions. Ito only stayed there until 1969 and opened his own office in 1971, calling it Urban Robot, which he changed to Toyo Ito and Associates in 1979. He won numerous Japanese architecture awards, participated in several competitions and exhibitions, both in Japan and internationally. Although he looked around himself with open eyes and took in much that was educational (Le Corbusier's ideas were important for him), he soon went his own way. He was critical of the formalism of the preceding generation and regarded this as anachronistic. Rather than pointing to a future that for him existed only in the present, he wished to direct people towards uncharted horizons.

As is the case with most young Japanese architects, Ito began with private buildings. His first was planned in his own office in 1971. A residential block, the Aluminum House was a wooden construction divided into two compartments, completely covered by aluminium in strips. It is a highly compact structure, from which

the floating lightness of later buildings cannot be predicted, although some of the qualities of his tent-like constructions may be detected in the outer structure. Other elements also predict his later projects – the complicated lighting, for example. Light comes through side windows at diverse heights and above all, through two large extensions (like chimneys or towers), so that two centres are created inside the house. This project was followed by further, small buildings.

Ito's architectural thinking became clearer with the White U residential building in 1976. Even though the closed concrete structure makes it appear rather like a fortress, the play of light is more consequential and somewhat more artistic. Soon afterwards, Ito received larger contracts for office buildings such as the PMT building in Nagoya (1978), that may be described as a building of curves with regard to its facade and interior. The aluminium facade appears like a mask and is curved like a wave with a slightly off-set axis. The higher part was added as a kind of 'faced' facade, and appears as if made from cut paper. The interior hall and stairway walls, partially made of glass bricks, are vaulted while the slim railings are curved and seem to sway like ropes.

These early works already revealed Ito's unwillingness to progress in a linear fashion. His starting-point was a blend of the physical form of the building site and his own theoretical considerations. For an outsider this results in an explicit interchange of formal and expressive articulation. If one regarded his development until then and only took into consideration the aspects of his work discussed here, it could be argued that his development led to dissolving the idea of 'space encircled by walls': a movement away from the enclosed quality of the Aluminum House and the White U towards the fluttering sails of the Noh theatre and the floating Nomadic Apartments. This would be a delusion as it is not Ito's goal. He is constantly searching for reality in urban life in a world he feels is simulated and unreal. He reveals great flexibility and constantly questions himself while adhering to his basic beliefs – this can be seen in the materials that best apply to his concept of poetically-articulated transparency and lightness: light, narrow metal supports, perforated aluminium and expanded metal sheets, glass, film foil bands and textiles.

The First Milestone: Silver Hut and Poetical Office Buildings

A first high point in his career and a turning-point in contemporary Japanese architecture is Ito's own house which he called Silver Hut (1984). Here he clearly realised his concept of transparency and lightness, combined with a relatively closed quality – poetry that can be seized in a concrete manner. The initial impression you gain in this house is one dominated by emotional reactions as if you had lived here for a long time, but you also have the feeling of being lifted away. The unusual atmosphere appears magical – is this Klingsor's garden? Ito himself called it 'garden of the winds'. Surrounded by greenery, the building is placed at the back of the slightly inclining plot, so that it appears completely cut off from the outside. Supported by independent narrow concrete columns, each spatial compartment has a light barrel-vaulted roof of steel frames divided into rhombuses, that can be looked into from below. Six smaller barrel-vaults are grouped around the inner courtyard which is covered by the largest of these. Originally it was covered by movable tent canopies, half of which had to be adjusted due to weather conditions. The kitchen is to the left of the entrance with a glass-brick wall, behind this the bedroom and children's room on a slightly lower level, while a studio and a Japanese-style room are on the right. These blend in curiously well under the vaulted steel roof. Daylight enters through windows in the sides and small triangular windows in the barrel-vaulted roofs. The inner courtyard has classically grey tiles and forms the centre of the house (only separated from the living area by glass doors). Although open towards the garden side, it is protected by transparent aluminium strips with arched ends. Despite the unusual appearance of the house, it is free of all eccentricity, yet there are many architects also in Japan who appear to think it necessary to attempt unusual effects in designing their own houses.[22] Ito himself describes his house as a mixture of Japanese citizen and farm houses (*minka*) and a spaceship in the process of landing. In fact, this comparison is not entirely fitting. It is simply his own house, an Ito house *par excellence*.

Offices and other commercial buildings naturally present practical problems, and Ito solves these in characteristic fashion. The construction of the M Building, an office building in Tokyo-Kanda, proved particularly taxing due to an angular building site. Ito therefore developed a concrete construction, the facade of which appears like a monumental pattern made from diagonally divided squares, covered by a roof of numerous rhombuses. He again used glass, aluminium strips and expanded metal; the materials that create a transparent, almost poetical atmosphere in this utilitarian building. This idea was achieved even more strongly in the T Building in Nakameguro (1990). The glass facade is structured horizontally by means of opaque film strips; floating stairs in the interior and open, curved corridors in front of the offices with narrow, elegant steel tube railings add to the impression of lightness and transparency.

New Developments in Construction Concepts

The fact that Ito is not limited to these basic concepts can be detected in two projects completed in 1993 – an old people's home and a fire station, both in Yatsushiro, south of Kumamoto on the island of Kyushu. Here, where there was a relatively large amount of land, Ito developed a 'system of bars' as in a computer bar code. In the case of the old people's home he unconventionally opened these 'bars' by making semi-circular, elliptical or round cut-outs in the flat roof of the elongated building in order to give an impression of transparency even to the vertical elements. The inner side, with a part straight, part curved front, encircles a wide, half-open inner courtyard that allows for a variety of communication methods. This flat, elongated bar construction was also used in the case of the fire station. Two compartments were placed together in an L-shape with the inner lines also constructed in an arched manner: the building is placed on supports to accommodate the fire engines and other equipment.

Today certain basic forms, colours and other elements are becoming the trademark of an architect – perhaps more so than ever – and this is also the case with Ito. One can therefore clearly distinguish that he likes vaulting, triangles, rhombuses, oval and bow shapes, and light elegant curves that he even uses when designing walls. As far as colour is concerned, he has a preference for silver and yellow, combined with milky-white, and slightly toned-down shades of red, blue or green, although these are only used very sparingly such as on window-frames. Such preferences

do not stand in the way of his search for finding new ways and means of putting them into practice.

The Challenge of Landscape

Ito's basic concept – confrontation with nature – remains of great importance to him, yet the two Yatsushiro projects reveal a new development of this confrontation. While Ito was initially concerned with what was invisible and elusive in nature – wind and light – landscape has become more important to him in recent years: he has tried to include incorporate it into his architecture.

Initially, he believed landscape in the form of physical nature (earth and plants) stood in opposition to the city, technology and even to architecture. When he was commissioned to build a guest house for Sapporo Breweries in Hokkaido, he arrived at a new conclusion: 'everything changed – it was a significant project in my career.'[23] He describes himself as standing rather forlornly in the wide open landscape, being more accustomed to building on narrow plots of land more or less enclosed by neighbouring buildings. He finally decided to take up the challenge posed by the landscape, by half-burying his building in the earth and digging out a plaza in the form of a shell in front of it, using the remaining earth to create a small hill nearby. This work interested him greatly and he observed that it could determine the 'flowing' of people and winds. 'At this point' he stated, 'I felt that the relationship between architecture and nature or between architecture and its surroundings should be relative and flexible.'[24]

The building blends softly into the raised plaza. The rear side is covered by earth and grass so that it presents itself as a hill crowned by three ventilation towers, surmounted by swinging, wing-like elements. A tunnel provides access to the entrance hall, the 'gate' of which is a glass construction covered by an awning. Ito took up a variety of the play of light from White U once again.

This was his first attempt to unite building and landscape in this manner. In the case of the Yatsushiro Municipal Museum he continued the development of these ideas, although this building could be seen as a synthesis of preceding architectural concepts. This, the first public commission received by Ito's office, was completed in 1991 and belonged to the larger project, Art Polis set up by the Kumamoto Prefecture.[25] In the case of the museum, Ito once again seized the ideas of the artificially created hill and the integration of landscape and architecture. Three storeys and a mezzanine floor were required, however, that would have completely dominated the flat ground (the city was built on alluvial land in the seventeenth century), the park-like landscape, the old patrician house opposite and the castle ruins. Ito therefore sank the lower storey for the exhibition space into the earth, recycling the waste earth to create a hilly landscape completely covered by plants. The next storey for administration, visitors' gallery, and cafe was, on the other hand, constructed completely openly, consisting almost entirely of glass walls, narrow supports and light barrel shells that jut out widely, made of coloured, sealed, stainless steel. A similar barrel swings out as a pointed triangle on the north side. The wind theme has taken on an elegant form here. Ito created a narrow mezzanine floor on the south side to accommodate a studio, working room and other designated areas. Above this rises the main store-room, shaped cylindrically with an off-set, elliptical cross-section. This cylinder, which is surrounded by aluminium and stainless steel perforated panels, floats over everything like a sculpture. The form itself is unusual for a museum, as is the fact that it is floating freely in space, exposed to the air. Ito, however, reminds us that the oldest preserved art store, the Shoso-in in Nara,[26] was no different and that it was the air in this case that conserved works of art more than one thousand, two hundred years old. He is of course making a symbolic comparison. Arches and curves dominate the form of the outer space, following the rhythm of a landscape that appears natural but has been artificially created. The museum visitor therefore approaches on a curving, ramp-like flagstone path that is placed on small supports and raised above the ground. The plot of land itself has the form of a circular segment. All these features – the path, the light vaults of the roof, the cylindrical, elliptical element – appear to make the building swing, as if hovering: it rests on the hill like a many-winged bird about to fly away. Japanese architectural criticism regards this as a significant event and a criticism of the state of modern architecture in Japan and elsewhere. Ito has thus set standards not only for Japan but also 'for a world that has discovered that if man and nature do not live in harmony, both will cease to exist.'[27]

The confrontation with nature and its concrete reflection in forms will remain Ito's theme for a long time, if not forever. He will, however, constantly search for new ways to bring his ideas to fruition, applying them to any given situation. The Municipal Museum in Shimosuwa was completed in 1993: separated from the Suwa Lake by a street, only a very narrow, two-hundred-metre-long strip of land was available. Therefore Ito developed a creative concept from the lake itself – he designed a 'wave' rising higher and higher, then falling in a soft curve as if trying to return to the lake but prevented from doing so as if frozen by ice. This impression was strengthened by numerous very thin aluminium panels which form the outer layer of the building, making it reminiscent of a boat, lying with its keel facing upwards. The glittering of the aluminium panels answers the glittering of the lake. Ito has succeeded in creating a dialogue with nature in a highly impressive manner that is almost too concrete.

Foreign Experiences, Competitions, Urban Planning

In the meantime, Ito is often asked to take part in competitions, as was the case for his project for the new University Library in Paris. He designed the ceiling lighting in the auditorium of the Frankfurt Opera House, which led to the commission for a Kindergarten in Eckenheim. Here again he tried to incorporate ideas from earlier projects, for example setting parts of the building below ground level, but due to constrictions imposed by German laws the project lost much of its floating quality; an impression only worsened by its less than perfect execution. It is only in the interior that Ito's hand can be recognised more clearly, in the muted but cheerful colours, reminiscent of traditional Japanese colour concepts, and used as an unobtrusive but clear hint at Japanese aesthetics.

For some time Ito has taken interest in urban planning. In 1990 he took part in a competition for the renewal of Antwerp. In his project, he tried to develop the idea of bar code building and to expand it into an urban situation. The competition for Shanghai's Luijiazui Central Area proved to be of great interest for him, since it offered the chance to develop a new type of city which allows for the accumulation of information.

His self-willed, individual way of dealing with the problems of today's situation, marked by the rise of electronic information and the loss of direct existential experiences, opens up new perspectives for architecture. Ito may be seen within the context of other architects, both Japanese and Western, but that context is not really significant – no artist can escape the influence of his time, nobody can remain aloof from his social surroundings. Comparisons are not overly helpful, however, and in the case of a person like Ito seem utterly irrelevant: it is only his work that counts. To those of us not living in Japan it is also extremely interesting to see how Ito, while accepting and integrating new developments in technology into his work, is nonetheless able to fall back in many instances on the essential basics of his own culture.

Notes

1 To us, the fantastic side of traditional Japanese architecture seems to lie in the apparently wilful placing of the windows in a tea pavilion, or in the design of sliding-door handles, and in the richness of form and colour of carved ornamentation (eg the Thoshogu Shrine at Nikko).

2 Koji Taki, 'Towards an Open Text' in Sophie Roulet and Sophie Soulié's Toyo Ito, Architecture Monographs, Paris 1991, p16.

3 Tatami mat, made of woven straw. Its average measurements, 182 by 91 centimetres, based on human proportion, together with the average distance between pillars (182 centimetres), create the modulor for traditional Japanese architecture. Shoji windows or doors are made of wood lattice covered with Japanese paper washi.

4 Koji Taki, op cit, p6.

5 Toyo Ito, 'A Garden of Microchips – The Architectural Image of the Micro-Electronic Age', in JA Library 2 (English version), Summer 1993, p7.

6 Toyo Ito, 'Towards a Post-ephemeral Architecture', Interview with Toyo Ito by Roulet and Soulié, op cit, p104.

7 Toyo Ito, 'Architecture in a Simulated City', Architectural Monographs No 41 Toyo Ito, Academy Editions, p9.

8 Koji Taki, op cit, p12.

9 Koji Taki, op cit, p12.

10 Isamu Wakabayashi, born 1936, one of Japan's most important contemporary sculptors.

11 Toyo Ito, 'A Garden of Microchips' op cit, p11.

12 Toyo Ito, 'Towards a Post-ephemeral Architecture' op cit, p93.

13 Kitaro Nishida, Japanese philosopher, 1870-1945 in Japanische Geistewelt, O Benl and H Hammitz, Baden-Baden, 1956, p320

14 Chanoyu – the art of tea, an artistic tea gathering. The communication of the participants, the handling of the things and the room create a new work of art. Developed in the fifteenth century, finally formalised in the sixteenth century, it is of greatest importance to Japanese aesthetics and remains an important cultural factor to this day.

15 Toyo Ito, 'The Reality of Architecture in a Future City', in Transfiguration, catalogue for 'Europalia', Brussels, 1989.

16 The Japanese woman is very independent and self-assured. Today, many young Japanese women, especially in Tokyo, live alone and independently; among them many career women.

17 Toyo Ito, 'Towards a Post-ephemeral Architecture' op cit, p100.

18 Pao I for a department store in Tokyo-Shibuya 1985, Pao II for the Europalia Show in Brussels dedicated to Japan, from Transfiguration, Centre Belge de la Bande Dessinée, 1989.

19 The 'Ginza Pocket Park of Tokyo': 'A Message towards the city of the 90s'.

20 Toyo Ito, 'Towards a Post-ephemeral Architecture' op cit, p93.

21 The Metabolists were a group of Japanese architects founded in 1960 under the direction of Kenzo Tange. Members included Kiyonori Kikutake, Kisho Kurokawa, Fumihiko Maki.

22 Occasionally such houses, with their extreme contours, stairs leading nowhere, decoratively placed half-moon and triangular windows, are reminiscent of modernist package design rather than architecture.

23 Toyo Ito, 'Towards a Post-ephemeral Architecture' op cit, p101.

24 Toyo Ito, 'Towards a Post-ephemeral Architecture' op cit, p104.

25 Kumamoto Art Polis is a project of the Kumamoto prefecture. Under the direction of Arata Isozaki, apart from some established architects, some of them from abroad, mainly young architects were asked to plan and execute buildings needed for the development of the prefecture. The project included the whole area of the prefecture.

26 Shoso-in, the treasure house of the Todaiji Temple at Nara, dating from the early Nara period (710-794). An azekura log structure is erected on pillars around three metres high, on a stone base. Through the contraction and expansion of the logs, a natural system of ventilation was created. It houses treasures of the temple and the Imperial household, works of art and applied arts, all of which have been preserved in perfect condition. A new magazine building was erected a few years after the last war.

27 Kengo Kuma, 'An Unprecedented Gentleness Towards Nature' in Yatsushiro Municipal Museum, Toyo Ito, Tokyo 1992, p30.

PAGE 14: Shimosuwa Municipal Museum; ABOVE: Yatsushiro Municipal Museum, axonometric

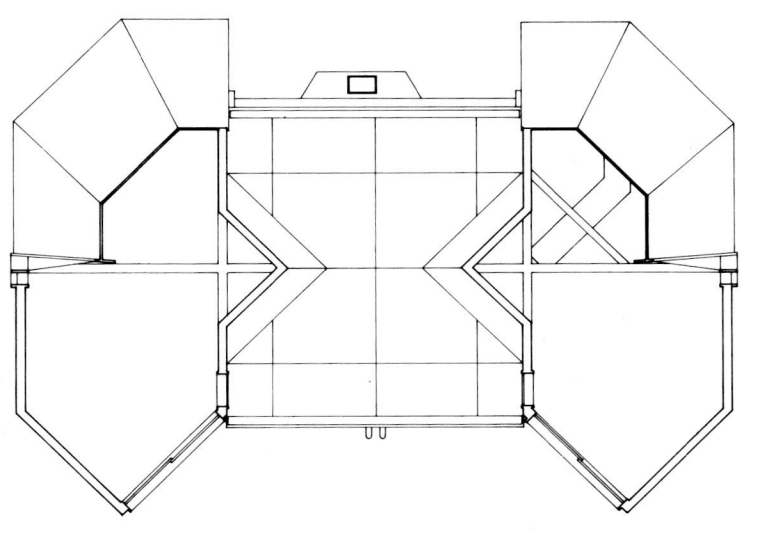 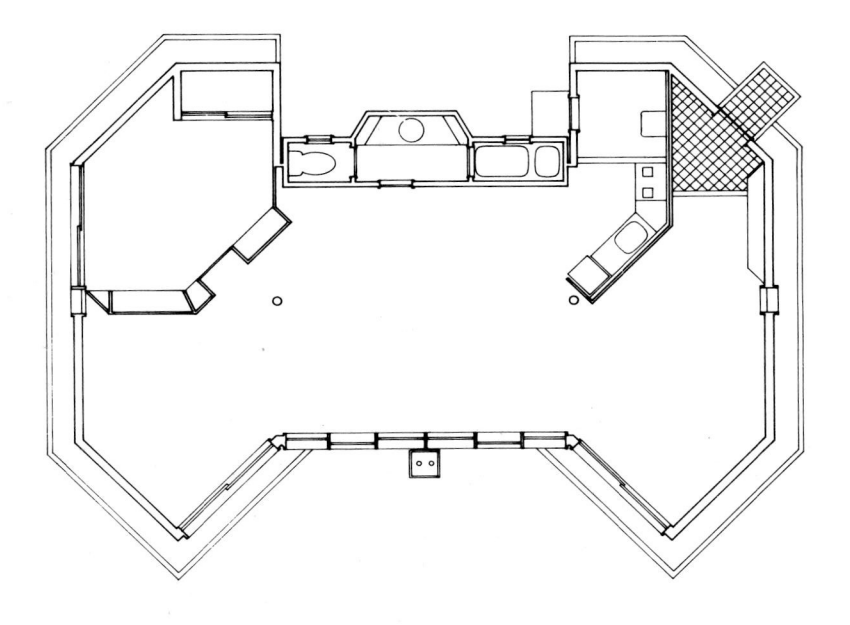

ALUMINUM HOUSE

Kanagawa, 1971

Ito's first project, this residential house is constructed of wood. It is located in a suburb of Tokyo. Beams form two main areas, by their perpendicular installation to two sturdy octagonal columns above. Shelters in a cylindrical formation cover these two spaces, which receive their light from above. Bedrooms and other private sections are constructed around these centres. A well of light results from these two central columns, allowing sunshine to pass through to the first floor. Stairs, constructed in the form of ladders in this well, lead to the second floor. The huge wooden frame of this building and sharply-pitched stairs, reflect the traditional Japanese house, but the external walls, covered by aluminium plates, resist this interpretation.

This was the first experimentation by Ito with metallic materials, which he continued to develop in later projects.

L TO R: Floor plans for first and ground floors

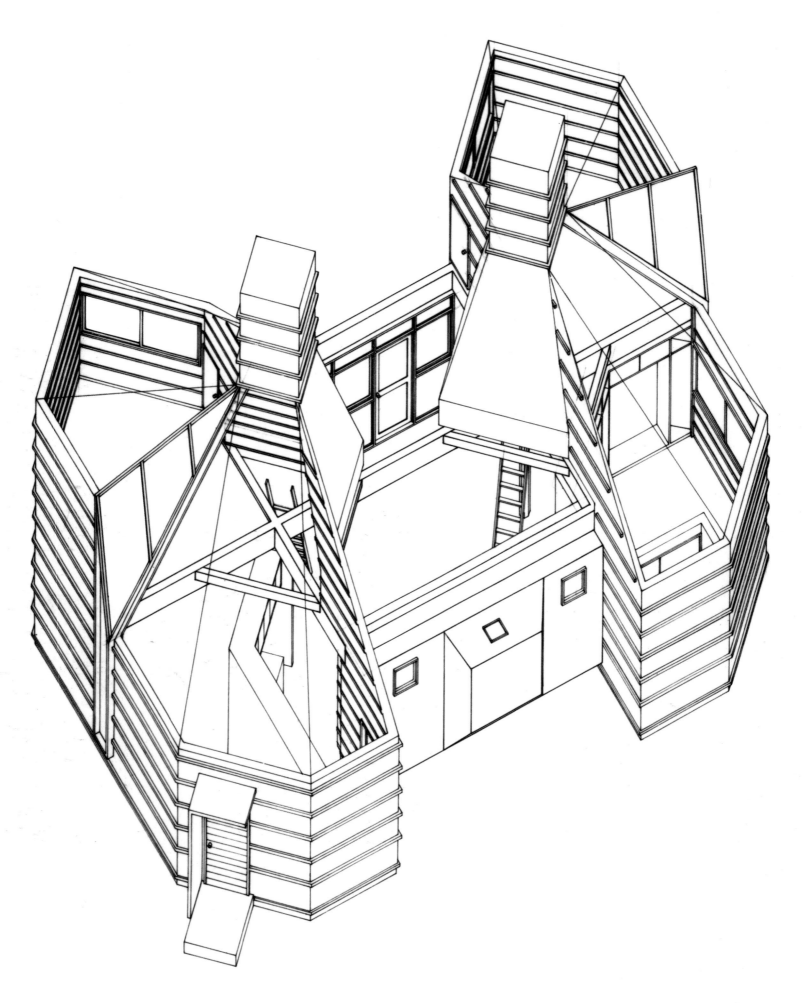

OPPOSITE: *Isometric*

PMT BUILDING

Nagoya, 1978

This building houses the Printing Machine Trading Company. Of the four storeys, the upper two are designated office space. The first floor is a showroom and repair workshop, where large printing machines are displayed; thus the ceiling is the height of two storeys (about seven metres). A mezzanine above forms an area for business matters. The main structure utilises a reinforced concrete frame, while flights of stairs, for example, stretch across this frame.

The aluminium facade expresses the essential character of the building. Staggering the axes of the volumes introduces mannerist instability and tremolo to the facade, which looks like a piece of paper fluttering in a breeze.

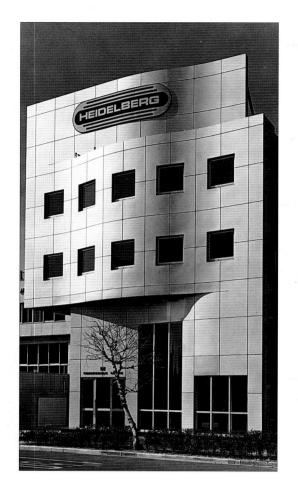

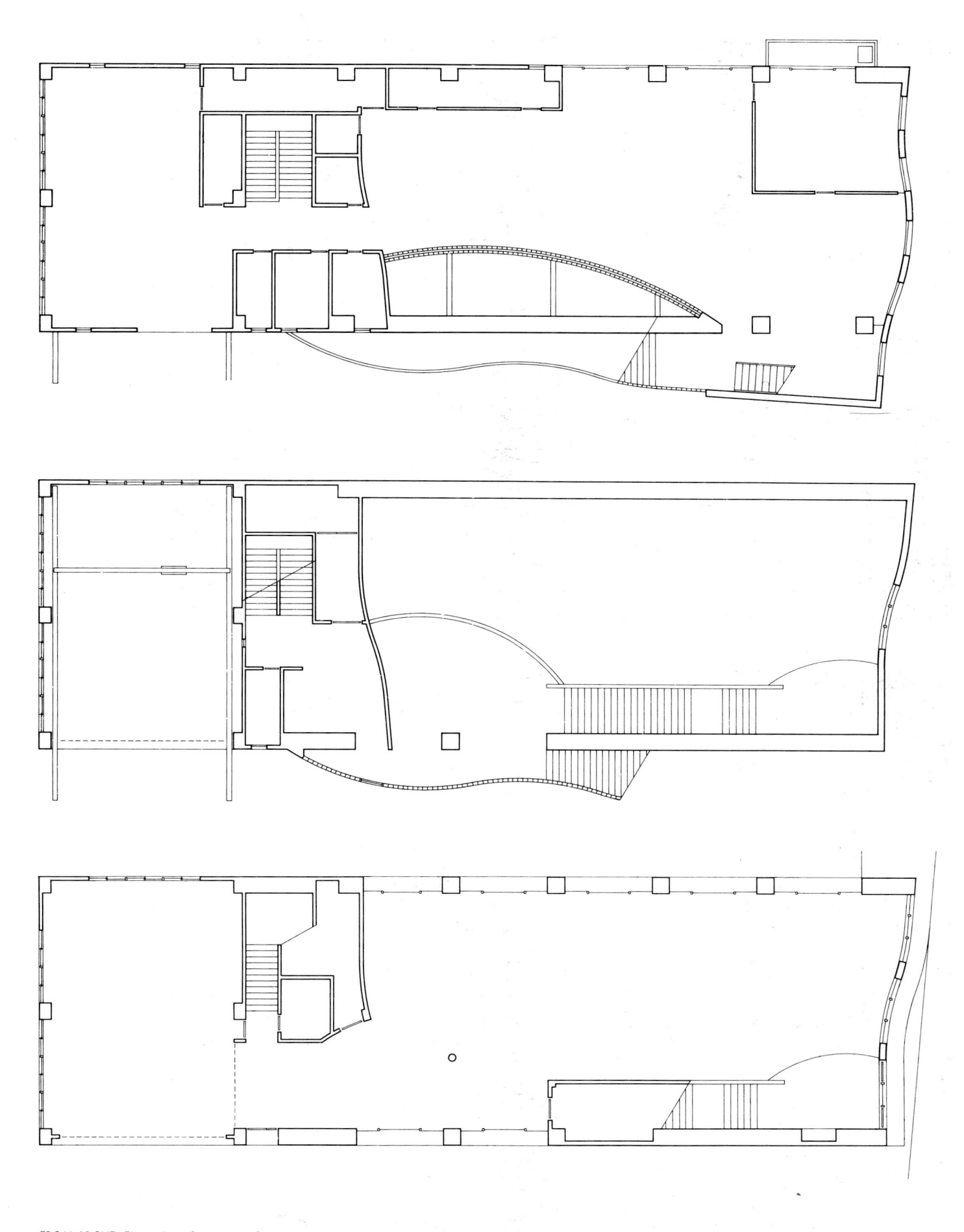

FROM ABOVE: Floor plans for second, first and ground floors

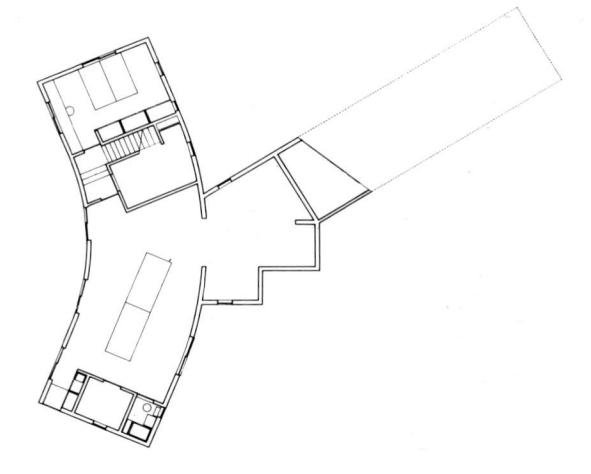
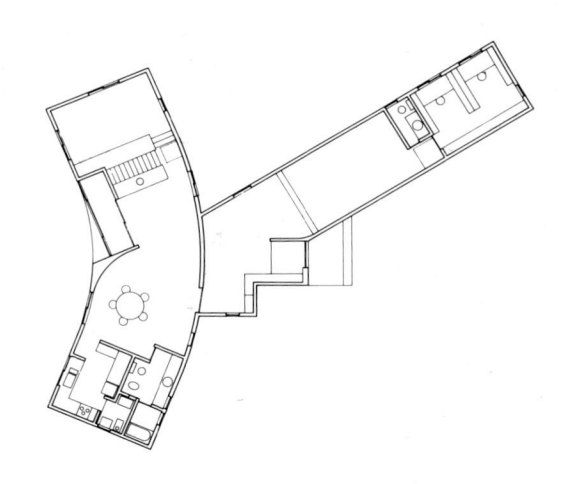

HOUSE IN KASAMA

Ibaragi, 1981

This house covers 290 square metres and utilises a 'two by four' wooden structural system. The T-shaped building slopes down towards the south: therefore the south wing is two-storeyed, while the north side consists of only one level. The two ridges intersect to form the entrance to the house. All external walls are enclosed by a flexible water-proof covering.

The house was designed to respond to the requirements of the client, a ceramic artist. It is divided into three practical sections – a small gallery under the north gable roof, which connects to the entrance; a studio and bedroom in the basement area of the south ridge; living space is on the upper floor. The house marks the progression from the seventies to the eighties. It has an area enclosed by walls like the earlier project White U, is centripetal and possesses a serious atmosphere, common in the former era. However, the house indicates clearly how architecture advanced into the eighties with the development of open plan and multi-centred spaces.

L TO R: Lower floor plan; entry-level floor plan

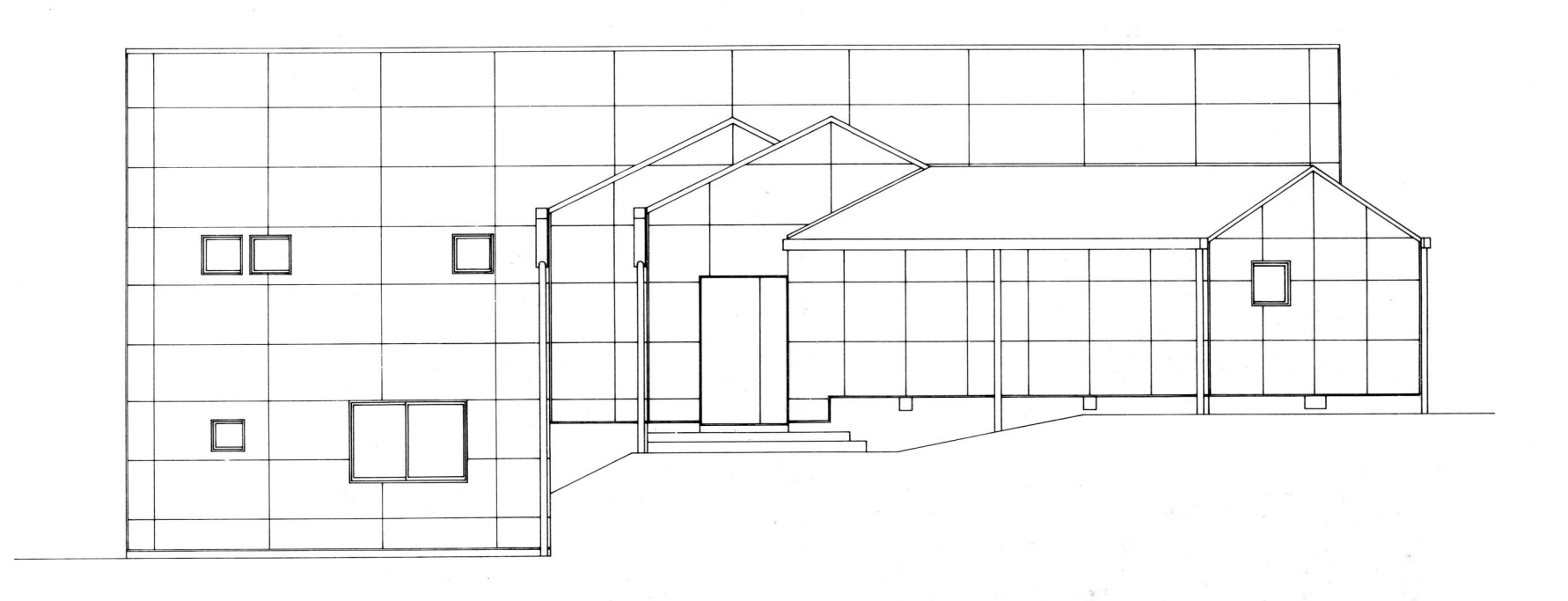

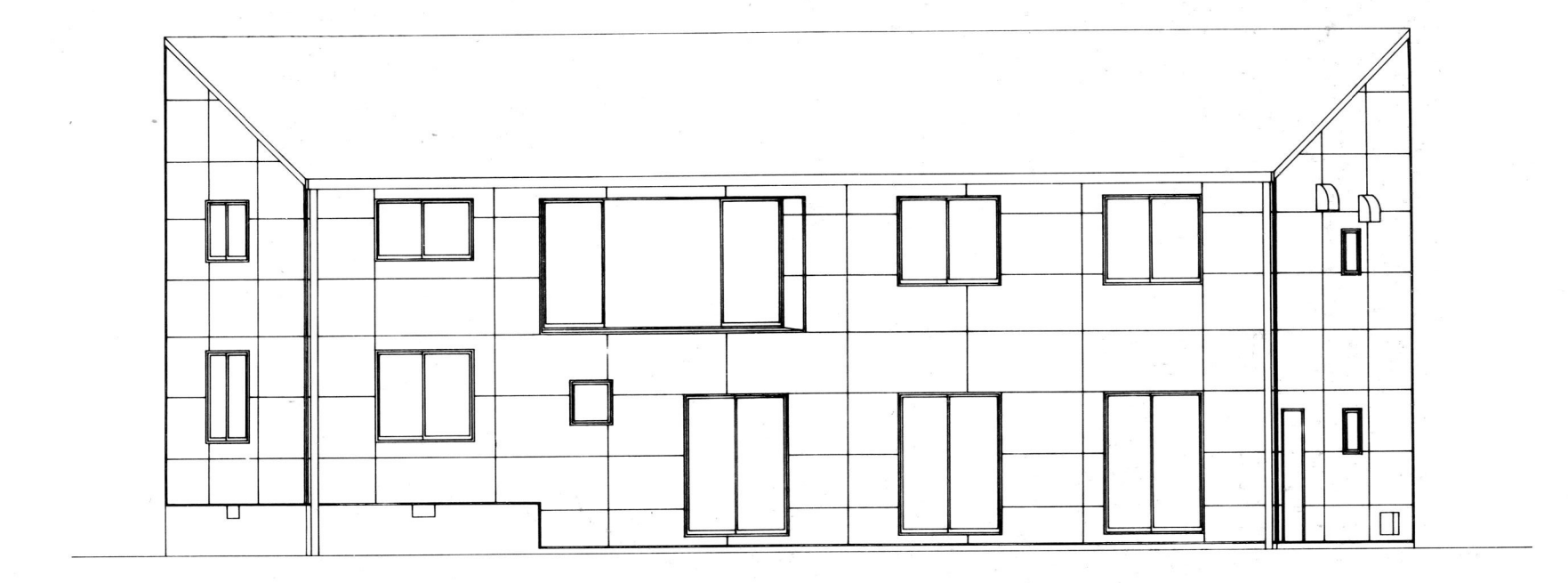

FROM ABOVE: North elevation; south elevation

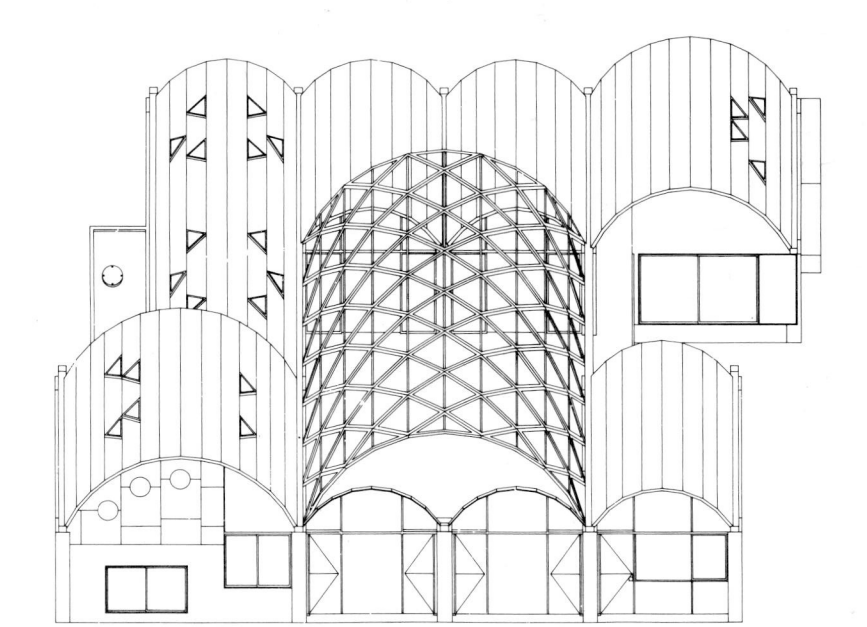

SILVER HUT

Tokyo, 1984

Silver Hut is just fifteen minutes by train from Shinjuku, and is located in a residential area in the centre of Tokyo. It is composed of a flat floor, concrete posts erected at 3.6 metre intervals, and a roof constructed of a steel frame with seven shallow vaults positioned over the posts. The gable runs from south to north.

A courtyard is accommodated in the centre of the south side, which is covered by a portable tent. This construction means that ventilation and sunshine are easily controlled. The courtyard is an almost exterior space which can be used for a variety of functions, according to the season and the weather. Along the western side are the utility room, kitchen and bedroom in the form of a concrete box half-buried underground, and a child's room above on a mezzanine.

The north side accommodates the dining area and living room, while on the east there is a study and Japanese room, each covered by separate vaults. Minimal walls, furniture or screens separate each room. The furniture is DIY or fashioned from old car parts: the fixtures throughout emphasise practical functions.

ABOVE: Axonometric; BELOW: Site plan including White U

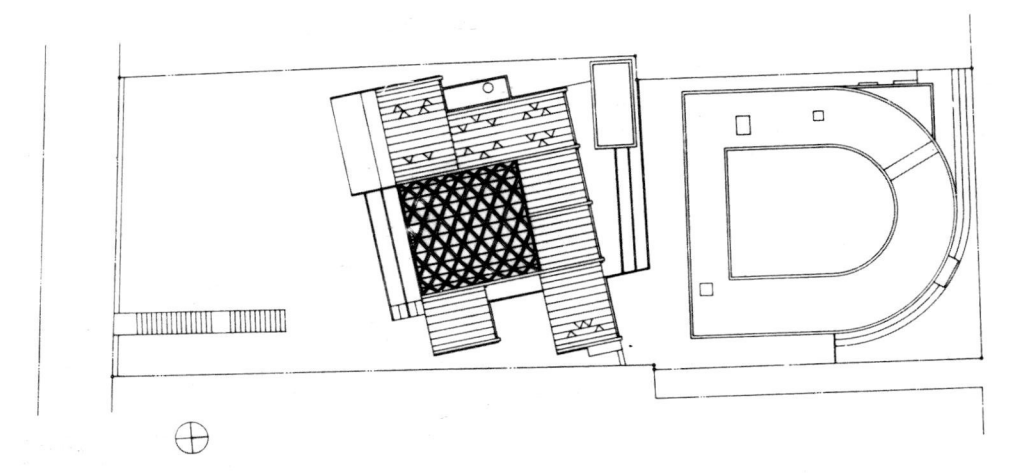

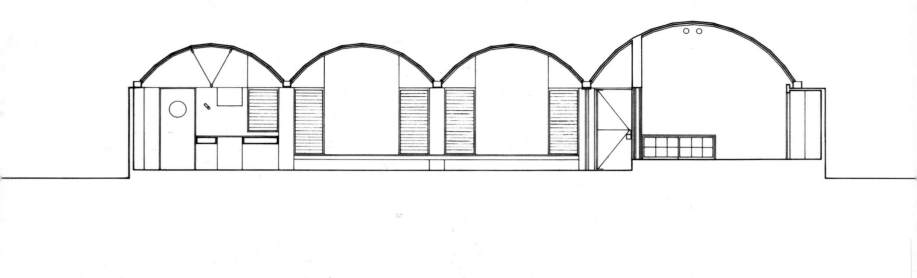

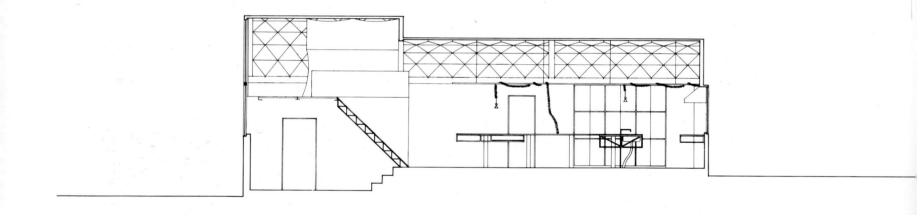

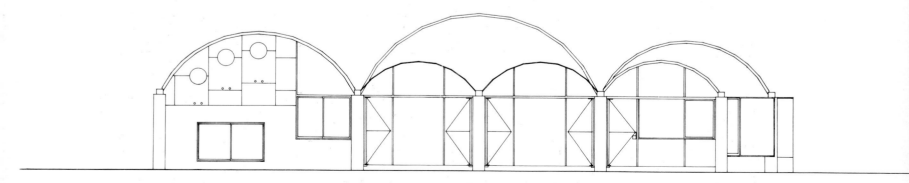

FROM ABOVE: Longitudinal section; cross section; south elevation

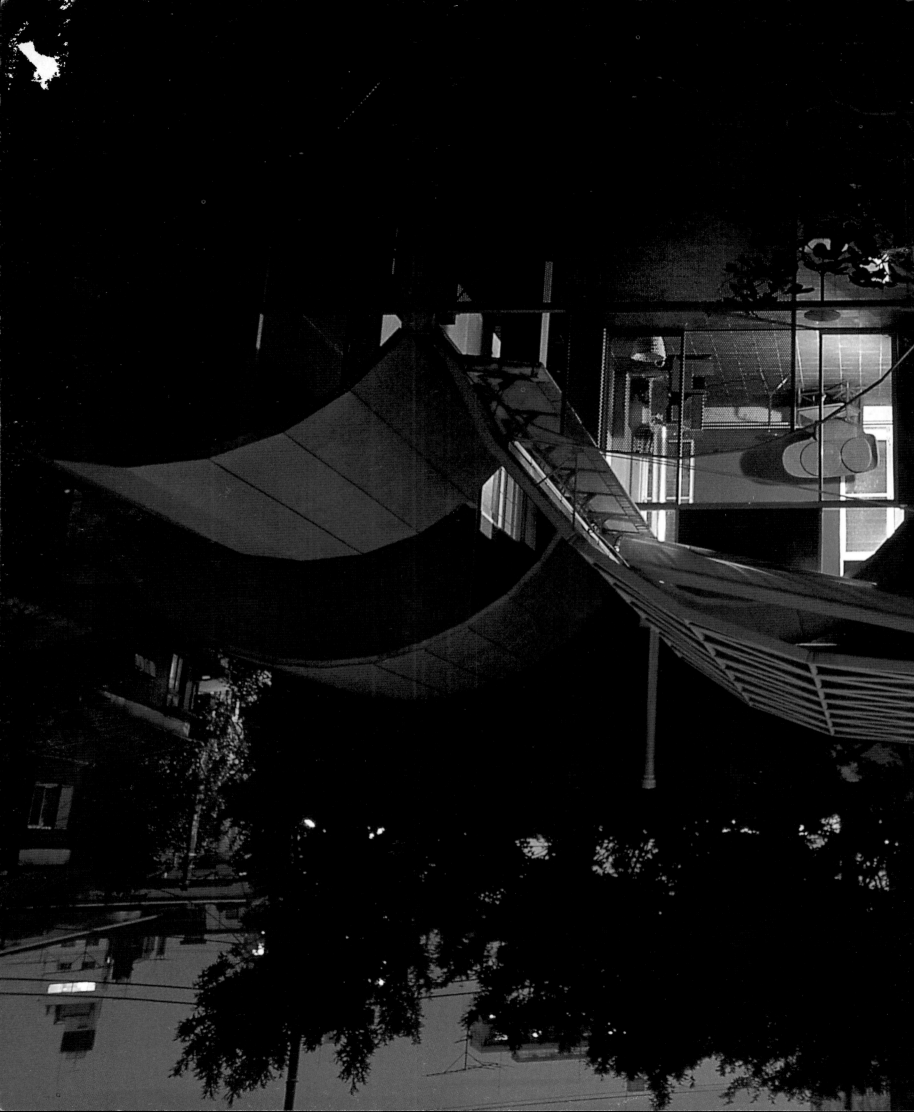

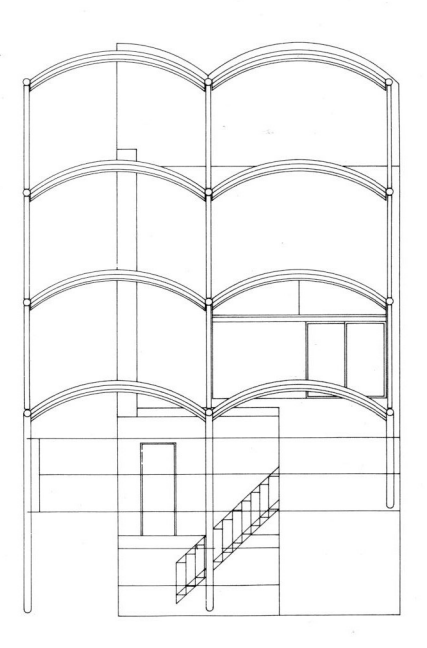

HOUSE IN MAGOMEZAWA

Chiba, 1986

A residential region close to Funabashi City, Magomezawa is approximately one hour by train from Tokyo. The house is constructed from reinforced concrete and steel, with the first floor utilising a concrete wall formation, with architectural concrete finish both inside and out.

Sunk just below ground level, the floor is finished with trowelled mortar, forming a concrete box enclosed by two vaults assembled with steel frames. A small bedroom below these vaults (approximately 20 square metres) is partitioned by sashes.

The construction allows light and wind to pass freely through the bedroom, in contrast to the kitchen and living room on the first floor. These are enclosed by concrete walls, but form two very different spaces, linked by a utility room and a terrace.

Galvanised steel panels are used for the facade, and form skin-like membranes which let in daylight and fresh air. These panels are similar to those found on building sites which protect areas temporarily closed to public access.

Sectional projection

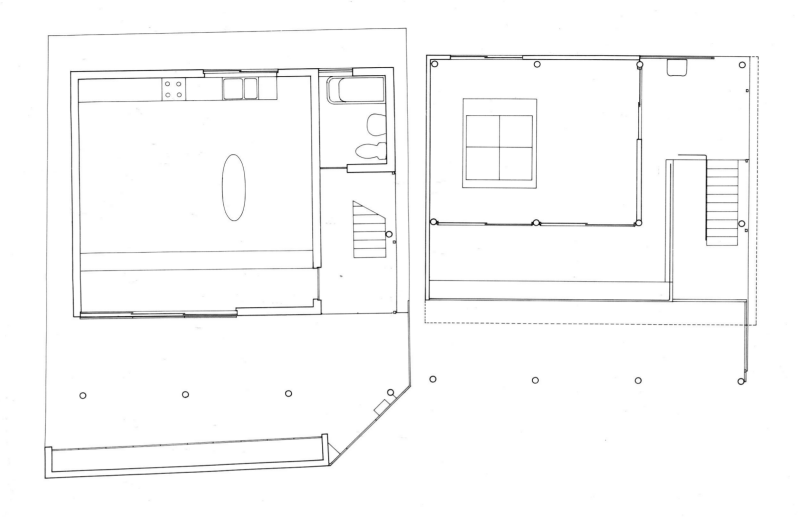

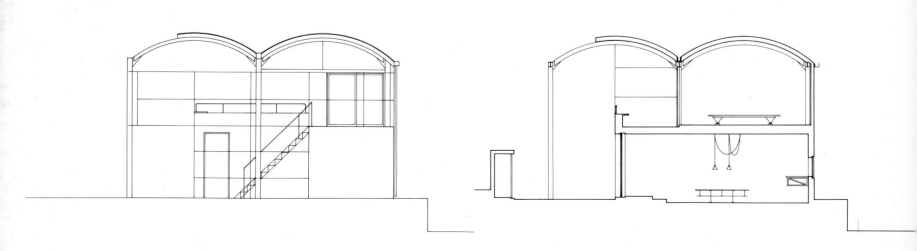

FROM ABOVE, L TO R: Floor plans for ground and first floors; Elevation; section

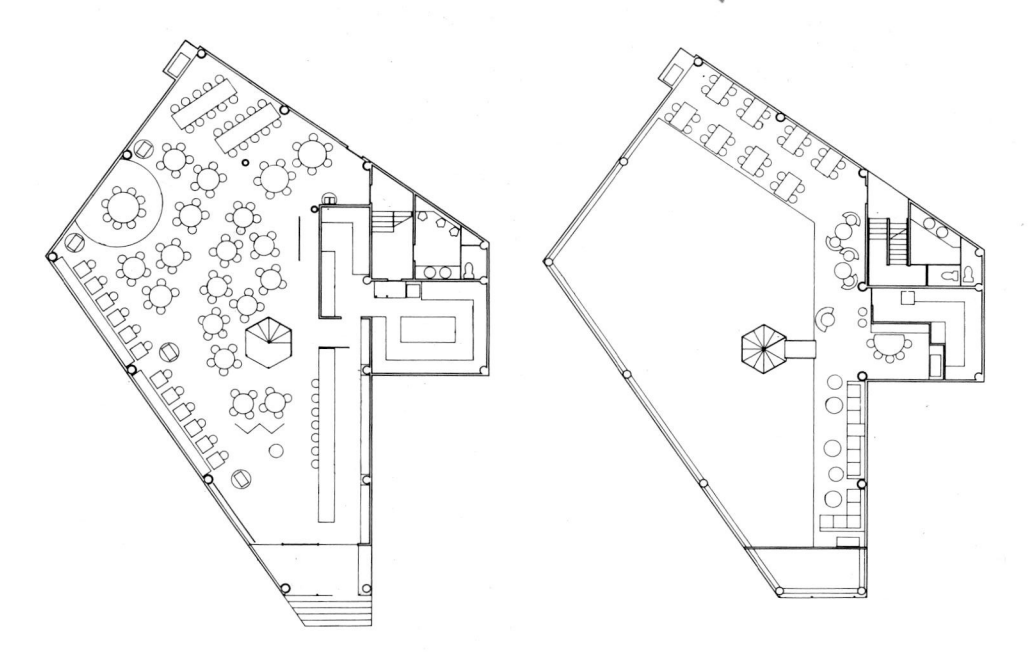

NOMAD RESTAURANT

Tokyo, 1986

Designed as a temporary structure to solve a planning delay, the Nomad restaurant and bar lies in Tokyo's most popular social area, Roppongi.

The atmosphere inside recalls the theatre, everything looks staged: from the entrance hall, fixtures and menu, to the waiters' clothes and the background music. The simple event of eating a meal and chatting with friends is transformed into a fictional and surreal affair.

Taking on the form of an enormous tent, the Nomad is an oasis for travellers in the 'desert' of Tokyo, and for those who live life on a whim. People are drawn in by the bright neon lights of the restaurant.

A steel frame construction ensures that possible building volume and height are maximised within planning regulations and expenditure restraints. Inside this frame float the main construction materials: fabric and perforated aluminium, which create the tent-like environment.

Resolutely, there is no architectural form – the tent-like building defies a consistent, determined design. The interior setting is filtered by a diffuse layer of finishes and furniture, effecting an illusory architectural quality. The diners appear to become nomads, seated at tables beneath metallic clouds fluttering in the artificial breeze.

ABOVE, L TO R: Floor plans for ground and first floors; BELOW: Section

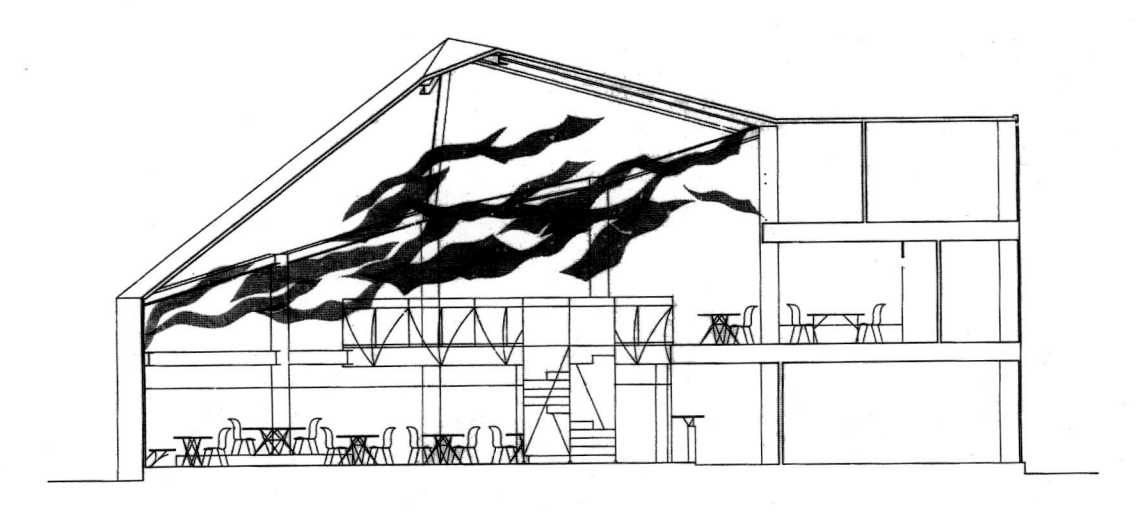

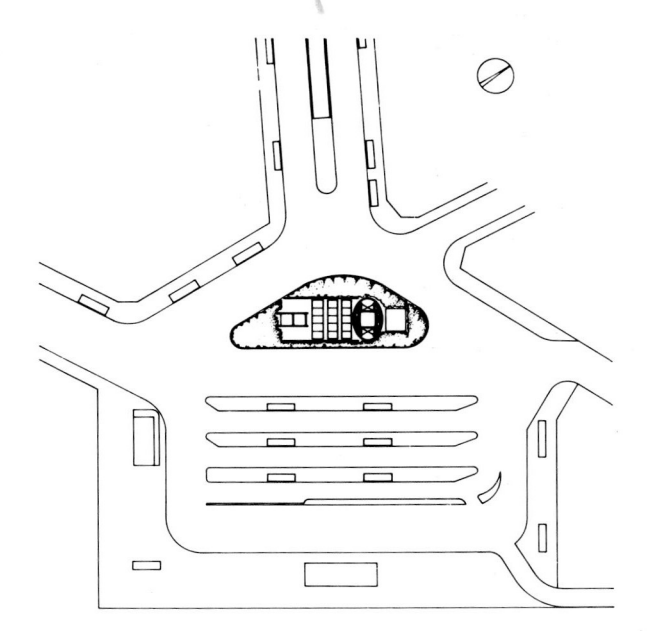

TOWER OF WINDS

Yokohama, 1986

A 21-metre high tower in the centre of a roundabout near Yokohama train station was covered in synthetic mirrored plates and encased in an oval aluminium cylinder. Floodlights positioned within these two layers, when lit, give the tower the appearance of a giant kaleidoscope.

The reflective properties of the aluminium panels emphasise the tower's simple metallic form during the day. At night the 'kaleidoscope' is switched on, presenting a brilliant display of relection upon reflection.

The tower consists of 1,280 mini-lamps and 12 bright-white, vertically arranged neon rings. Thirty computer-controlled flood-lights (24 on the interior, the remainder on the exterior) make patterns of light within the tower, according to the time of day. Natural elements such as noises, and wind-speed and direction affect the intensity of the flood-lights: the result is a controlled 'natural' phenomenon. The panels sometimes become a translucent film, at other times they appear to rise floodlit to the surface.

Site plan

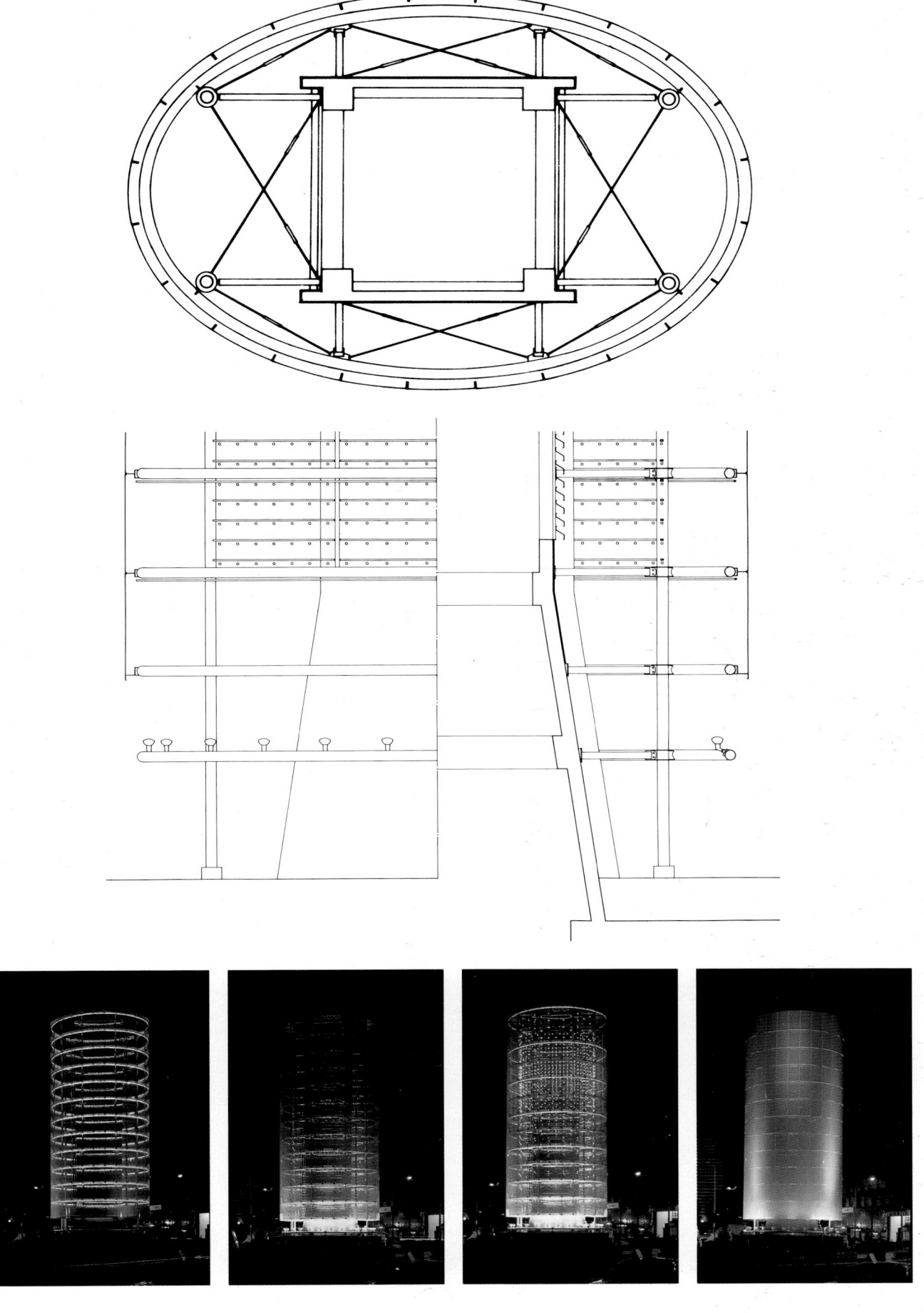

FROM ABOVE: *Plan; detail*

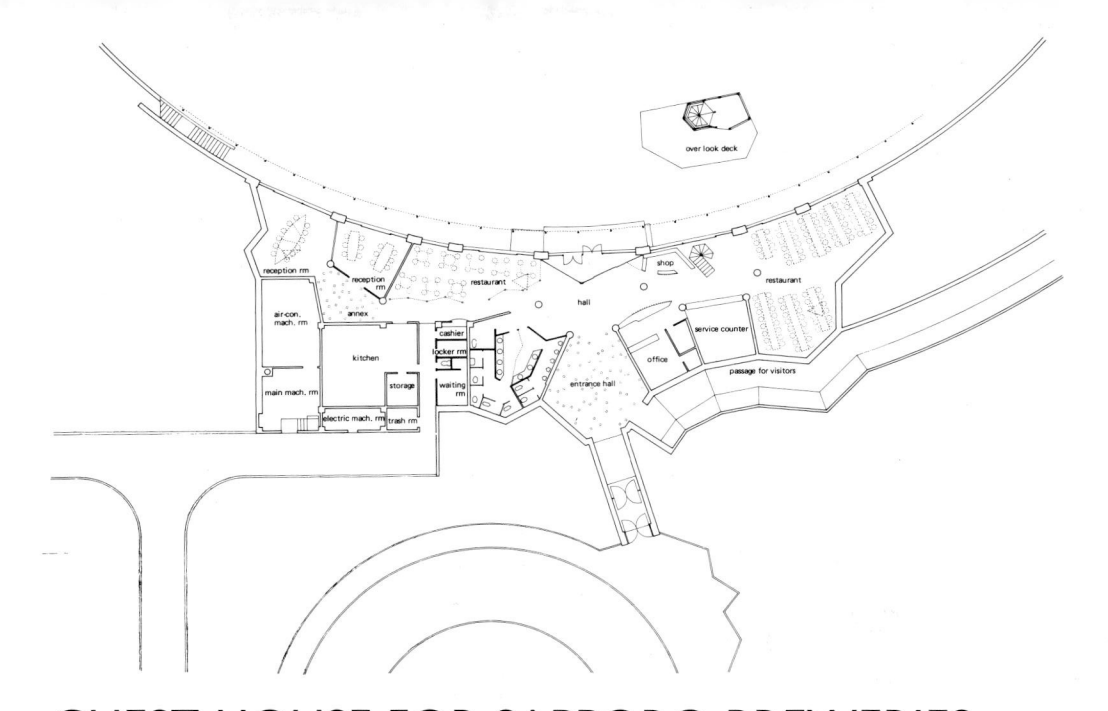

GUEST HOUSE FOR SAPPORO BREWERIES

Hokkaido, 1989

Sapporo Breweries is a vast plant, covering 300,000 square metres, on the main route between Chitose Airport and Sapporo City. In order to accommodate visitors to the plant, a guest house was built in the garden which comprises one third of the entire site.

The guest house appears along the path from the site entrance to the garden, which contains the Pond of Odin, the Hill of Elm Trees, Fairy Wood, the Plaza of Fire and Marshland in the Image of a Scandinavian Landscape. Across from a sunken garden lies the guest house, also buried, to fuse its form with the surrounding topography. The house resembles an earthwork more than architecture.

Unit spaces are created by polygonal forms: each is assigned a function – bar, restaurant and guest room. Skylights, textiles and frescoes are concluding features. Taken as a whole, the design (incorporating ventilation tower, skylights and entrance canopy) has the appearance of aeroplane wings. The walls around the plaza are shielded by perforated metal screens to soften the otherwise harsh character of the guest house.

Floor plan

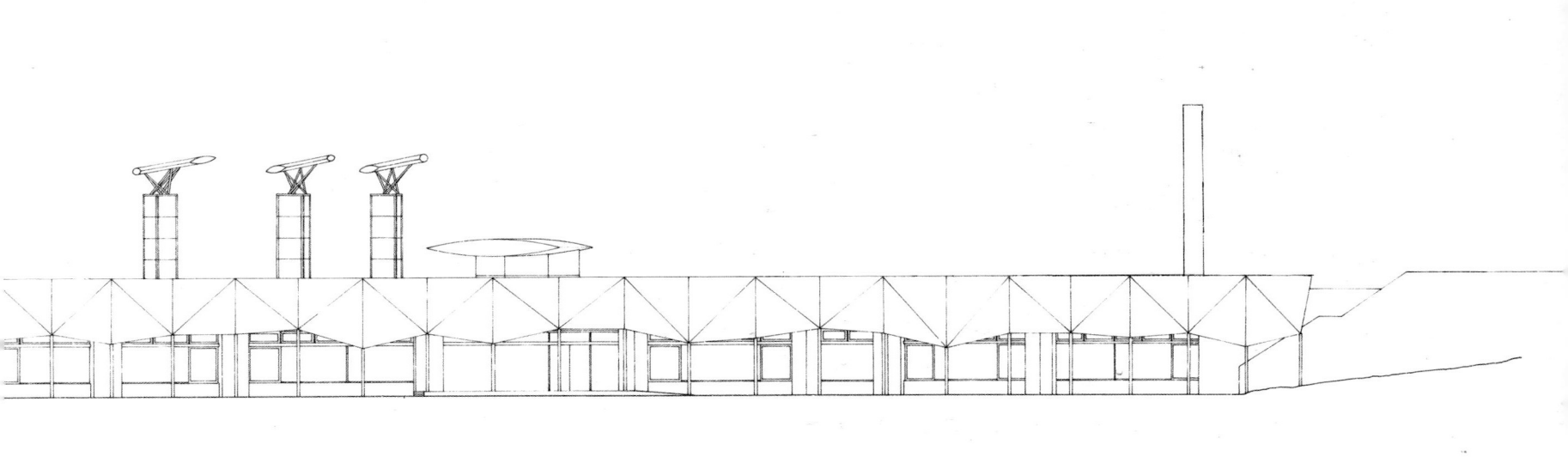

Elevation from plaza

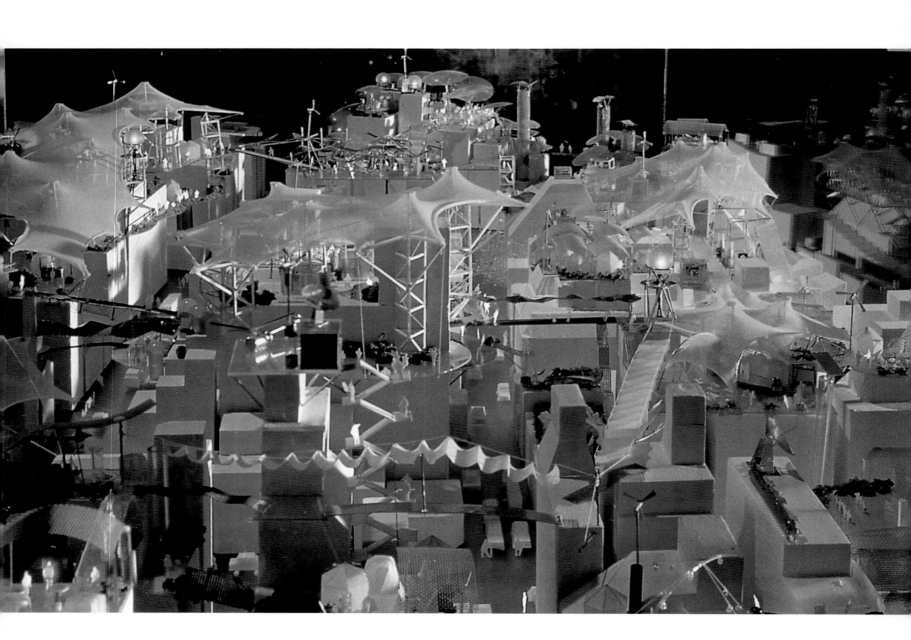

ROOF GARDEN PROJECT

Tokyo, 1988

This project was prepared for an exhibition and intended to 'recompose' the roofs of several buildings in the old town sector of Tokyo. This extremely dense area has been developed since the Edo era, and is composed of small blocks of flats. The most spectacular areas of these buildings are the roof spaces, where people can enjoy the sunshine and breezes, the sunset and the moonlit sky.

On the roofs, cooling towers and water tanks make way for a kindergarten, facilities for the elderly, meeting and sports areas, restaurants and cafes. These would be constructed as extensions to the buildings rather than separate entities; the whole covered by a membrane to protect people from the climate. The different territories are connected by bridges, creating a pedestrian network in the air.

Compared to the chaos of the traffic jams and masses of people below on the street, this project envisaged an airborne paradise, suspended ten metres above the ground.

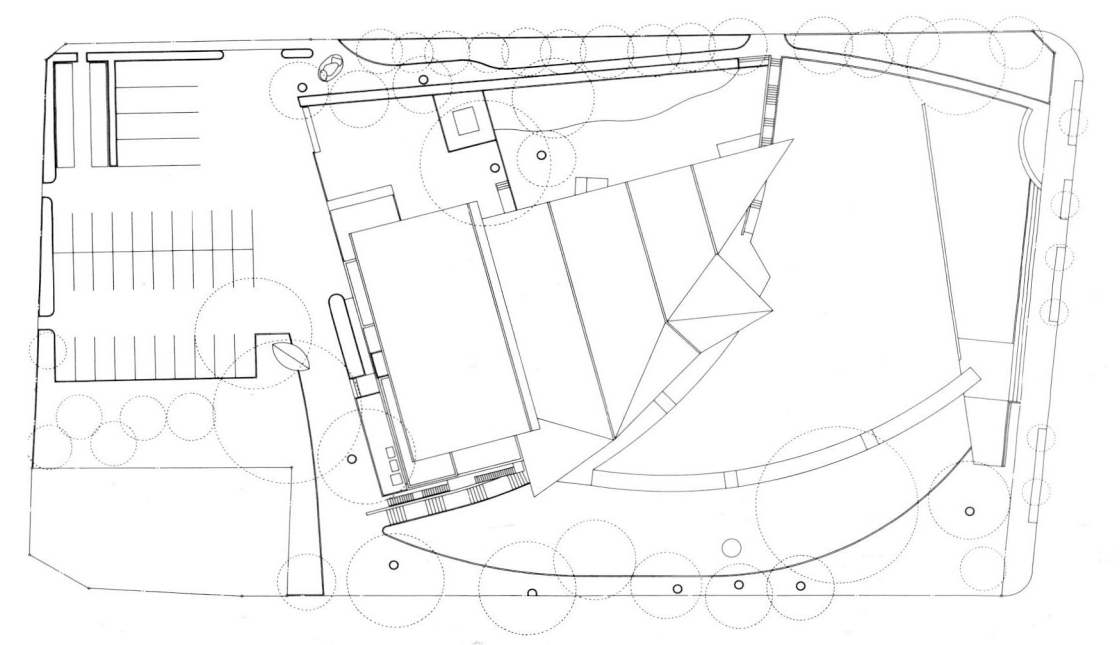

YATSUSHIRO MUNICIPAL MUSEUM

Kumamoto, 1991

Yatsushiro Municipal Museum was one of the first major projects for the Art Polis programme organised by the Kumamoto Prefecture. The programme, which was the idea of Kumamoto Prefecture and Arata Isozaki, aimed to co-ordinate the work of architects to make the Prefecture a cultural and architectural centre. As a result, the city of Yatsushiro wished to build a new museum to house under one roof its many historical artefacts, previously stored in several different locations, which would contribute to establishing Yatsushiro as a cultural centre in Kyushu.

The museum is situated in a historical area near the old moat of the now dilapidated Yatsushiro castle. Opposite is Shohin-ken, an Edo period villa of the Matsui family who governed the area at that time. The first impressions of the site are the low, horizontal profile of Shohin-ken and the flatness of the leafy site itself. This, added to the request that as many as possible of the existing trees be preserved, gave rise to

the idea of the new museum as a park. Lessening the building volume and maintaining a park-like atmosphere seemed the most appropriate response to a site of this nature. A major problem was that the museum criteria and the ratio of building to site area required at least three storeys. Efforts were concentrated on achieving this criteria without completely overshadowing the villa. The main concern in the process of this design was to avoid the massiveness predomi-nating the conventional museum and to create more light and bright space.

Thus the largest space, the main exhibition hall and machine room, was placed on the first floor and covered by an artificial hill. Because the ground floor is submerged, the first floor appears at ground level. A curved ramp runs over the hill and alongside a wall which gives a feeling of continuity with the natural plane of the landscape. There is an excellent view over the hill down to the street and you can sense the extension of the building into

the landscape. The third floor is a hovering cylinder above the multi-vaulted roof of the main building comprising artefact storage. In contrast to conventional museums where storage is located out of sight, the aim was to show that a museum stores artefacts as well as exhibiting them – elevated storage was traditionally found in Japanese Shoso-in.

Different structural systems were used in response to the purpose of each space. The first floor has the minimum ceiling height possible to conserve space. A steel frame multi-vaulted roof covers the second floor to provide light. The rear of the building consists of a rigid reinforced concrete frame structure. By combining these different structures and spaces, the attempt was made to create a museum where people can enjoy not only the artefacts but also the building itself.

Site plan

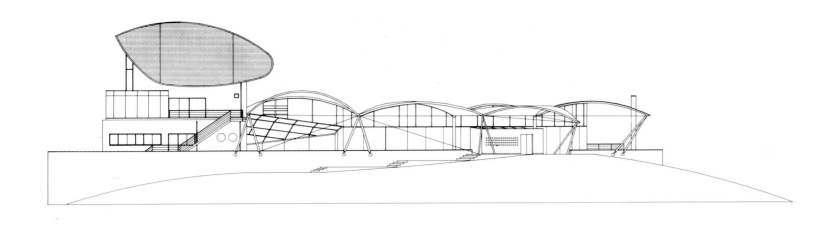

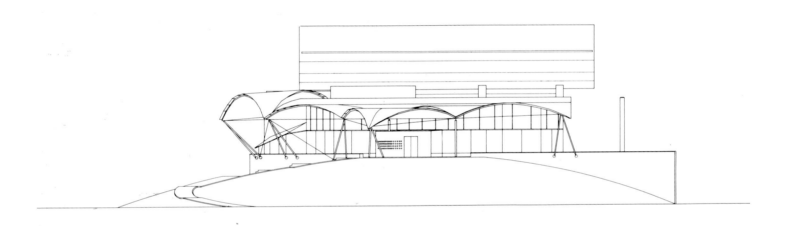

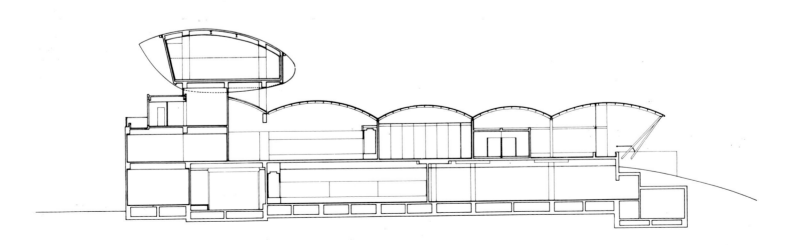

FROM ABOVE: East elevation; north elevation; section

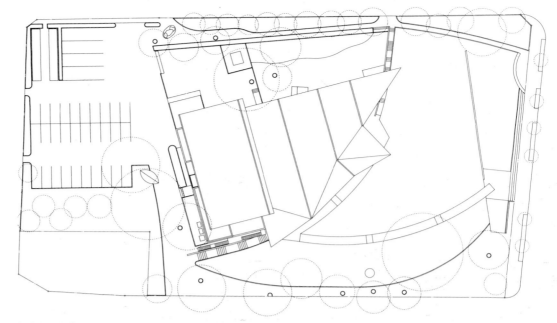

YATSUSHIRO MUNICIPAL MUSEUM

Kumamoto, 1991

Yatsushiro Municipal Museum was one of the first major projects for the Art Polis programme organised by the Kumamoto Prefecture. The programme, which was the idea of Kumamoto Prefecture and Arata Isozaki, aimed to co-ordinate the work of architects to make the Prefecture a cultural and architectural centre. As a result, the city of Yatsushiro wished to build a new museum to house under one roof its many historical artefacts, previously stored in several different locations, which would contribute to establishing Yatsushiro as a cultural centre in Kyushu.

The museum is situated in a historical area near the old moat of the now dilapidated Yatsushiro castle. Opposite is Shohin-ken, an Edo period villa of the Matsui family who governed the area at that time. The first impressions of the site are the low, horizontal profile of Shohin-ken and the flatness of the leafy site itself. This, added to the request that as many as possible of the existing trees be preserved, gave rise to

the idea of the new museum as a park. Lessening the building volume and maintaining a park-like atmosphere seemed the most appropriate response to a site of this nature. A major problem was that the museum criteria and the ratio of building to site area required at least three storeys. Efforts were concentrated on achieving this criteria without completely overshadowing the villa. The main concern in the process of this design was to avoid the massiveness predomi-nating the conventional museum and to create more light and bright space.

Thus the largest space, the main exhibition hall and machine room, was placed on the first floor and covered by an artificial hill. Because the ground floor is submerged, the first floor appears at ground level. A curved ramp runs over the hill and alongside a wall which gives a feeling of continuity with the natural plane of the landscape. There is an excellent view over the hill down to the street and you can sense the extension of the building into

the landscape. The third floor is a hovering cylinder above the multi-vaulted roof of the main building comprising artefact storage. In contrast to conventional museums where storage is located out of sight, the aim was to show that a museum stores artefacts as well as exhibiting them – elevated storage was traditionally found in Japanese Shoso-in.

Different structural systems were used in response to the purpose of each space. The first floor has the minimum ceiling height possible to conserve space. A steel frame multi-vaulted roof covers the second floor to provide light. The rear of the building consists of a rigid reinforced concrete frame structure. By combining these different structures and spaces, the attempt was made to create a museum where people can enjoy not only the artefacts but also the building itself.

Site plan

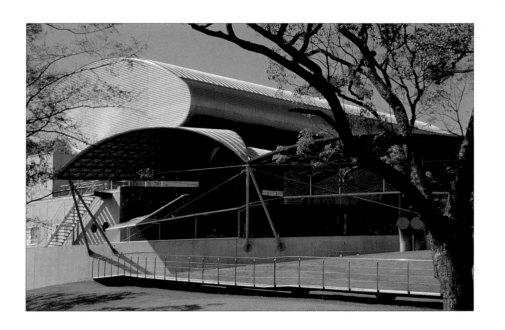

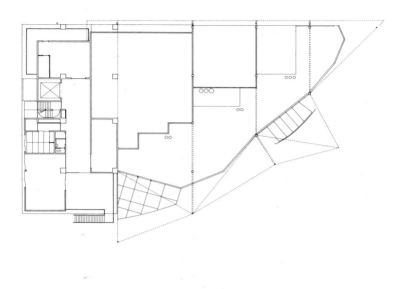

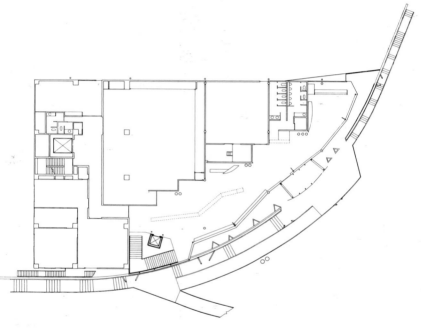

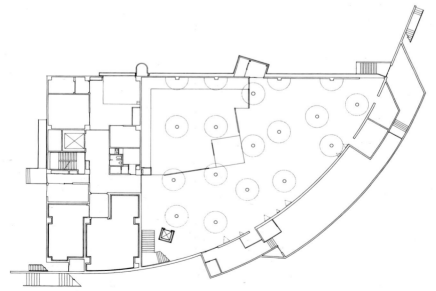

FROM ABOVE: Floor plans for second, first and ground floors

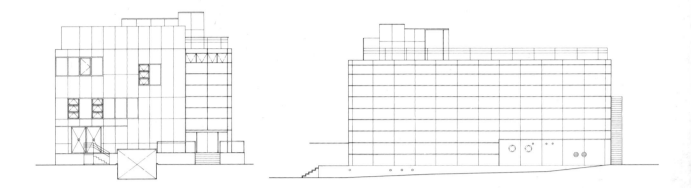

T BUILDING IN NAKAMEGURO

Tokyo, 1990

Situated between commercial, industrial and residential areas, this project stands between tall buildings and family housing. Along the boundary with the street is a 'skin' made from a milky film substance attached to a long screen. The areas designated for offices are amalgamated in one location, so that they are easily adaptable for various purposes as necessary. Between this area and the screen is a 'void' area covering three storeys, which contains 'hovering' services: toilet booths are suspended from the ceiling, as are the stairs, deck slabs and glazed steel lift shaft. People only stay here for a short time, and so it is filled with a sense of constant flux.

The screen blurs the concept of inside and outside: the one permeates into the other. This void seems at times an assimilated part of the building, but at others appears completely separate. It illustrates the illusion of 'reality', in the same way as an aquarium provides us with a 'natural' environment.

This building harmonises the perceptions of architecture and landscape. The light nature of the structure reveals an evanescence amidst the constant fluidity and chaos of the city.

L TO R: North elevation; west elevation

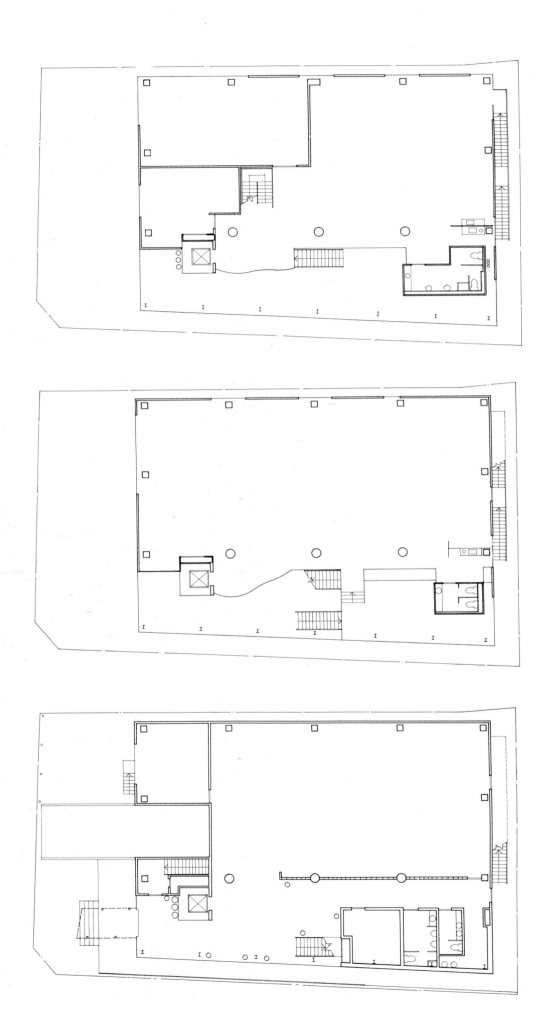

OPPOSITE, FROM ABOVE: Floor plans for second, first and ground floors

OPPOSITE, FROM ABOVE: Floor plans for second, first and ground floors

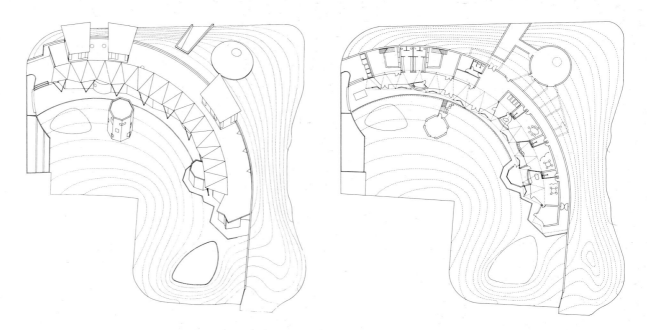

PUBLIC KINDERGARTEN IN ECKENHEIM

Frankfurt, 1992

Eckenheim is a residential area in the northern part of Frankfurt. This project reflects the original brief to keep the structure close to the ground, covering as much of the site as possible: the intention was to incorporate the building into the landscape.

Tree-like columns form a base, over which is suspended a triangular roof made from folded plates. This was achieved by enclosing a wooden frame with sections of plywood. Support was provided by diagonal steel-pipe brackets.

The general ethos of the school is to provide day-care for the children of working parents, rather than nursery education. A central entrance hall divides the main rooms to the left and right: access for the nurseries is along the wall, while the kindergarten is reached from the garden. The

classrooms are surprisingly different from one to the next: each makes interesting use of skylights, wall alcoves, and floor levels, providing the children with numerous environments to explore.

The concept of the kindergarten has less to do with that of a house, yet it is a place where the children can live comfortably. A nurturing atmosphere is created by the sculpted environs, and elements such as the light wooden roof, curved walls, octagonal library and circular hall either have a floating quality or are buried within the building. The kindergarten is an attempt to realise landscape architecture.

L TO R: Axonometric; site plan

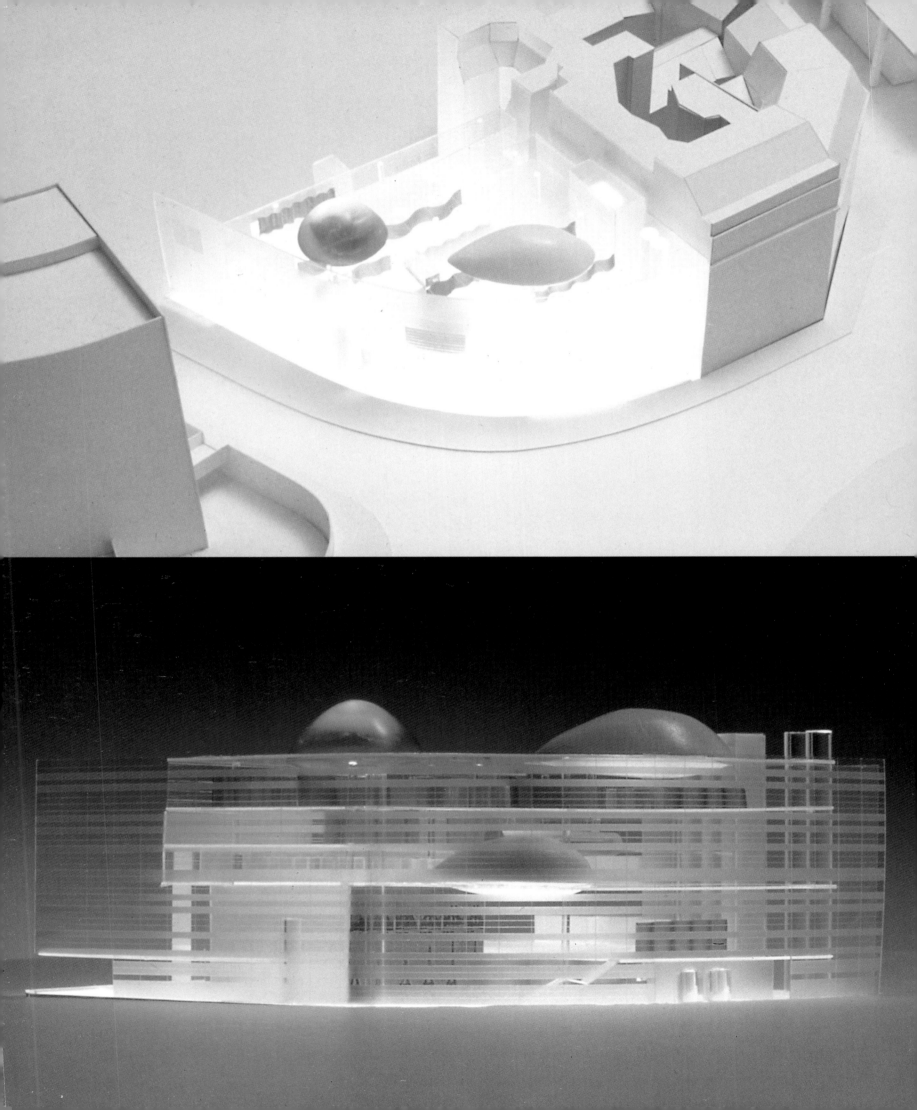

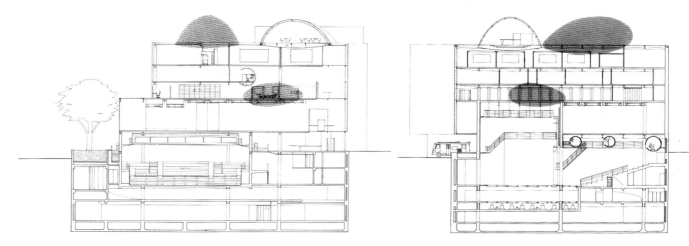

JAPANESE MAISON DE LA CULTURE

Paris, 1990

Designed as a competition project for the Japanese Maison de la culture in Paris, 'Media Ships floating on the Seine' – as this project is known – is located in an area not far from the Eiffel Tower by the Seine, which accommodates both traditional Parisian terraces and contemporary buildings.

Influential to the design was the image of a spaceship drifting in from Tokyo to despatch information and culture. This is inherent in its skin-like facade made of electronic crystal glass, behind which are floating many functional spaces and facilities.

Behind this 'skin' lie three 'bubble' shapes wrapped in a permeable skin like nuclei in cells. They possess particular functions in response to human needs such as learning, talking, socialising and eating and are situated in the academic zone of this building. Thus an information 'control room' hovers in this library space, while two other bubbles – the VIP room and a restaurant – hover in or near the roof, commanding panoramic views over the city. A variety of images can be reflected on the restaurant's glass facade, thereby rendering a theatrical space. Like skin or screens, floors and walls are indicators; all spaces are temporary, having originated from the information emitted.

This project indicates how a unique form of architecture is able to evolve, through engaging individualised symbols with a soft, transparent entity.

L TO R: Section across auditorium; section through auditorium

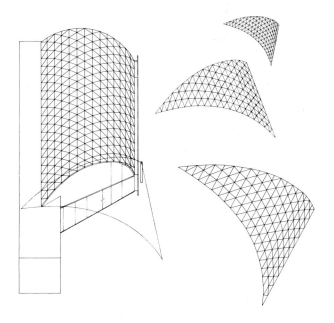

GALLERY U IN YUGAWARA

Kanagawa, 1991

The programme for this building was to create store and exhibition rooms. This led to a simple building which is closer to a storehouse rather than a gallery. The materials used are very simple: exposed reinforced concrete, mortar and steel. From an early design stage the basic scheme was to anchor the storage space as a reinforced concrete box while the gallery space would be enveloped by a light vault. The original concept was of a calm empty space with softly changing colour tones – an almost natural setting brought alive by exhibits and people, which together form small, temporary spaces. These delicately created spaces seem best surrounded and wrapped by a light, thin vaulted roof.

Usually galleries have an introverted, closed feeling but in this particular case, considering its location and that it is a small private gallery, it does possess a great deal of openness.

Only the exposed concrete-finish side wall of the storage box works as a wall for display while other enclosed sides of the gallery space are almost inexistent, overshadowed by the vaulted roof. From the skylights above and the two side openings the wind sways through the space and gentle natural light shifts smoothly across the gallery, forming a continuity between it and the terrace: there is a diagonally-placed double glazed door made from perforated aluminium and the floor has a mortar finish both inside and out. When artworks or furniture such as chairs are placed on the terrace the relationship between interior and exterior is strengthened and the intention behind this building becomes apparent.

Axonometric

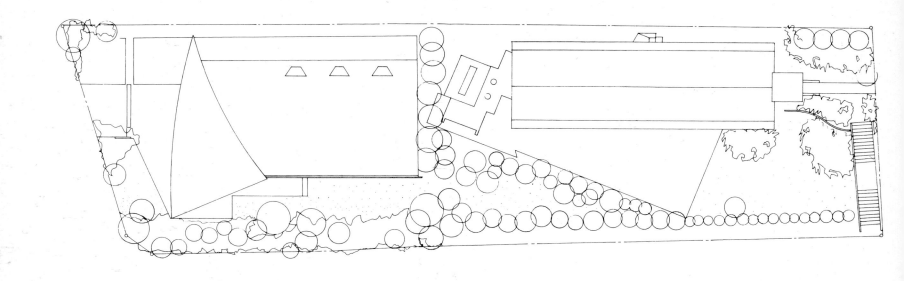

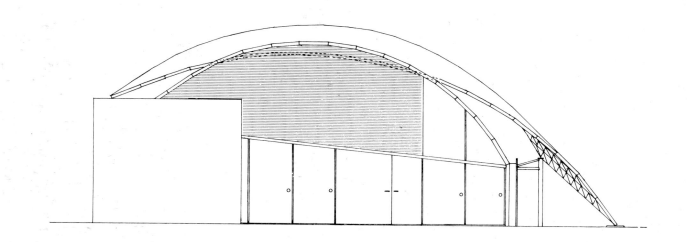

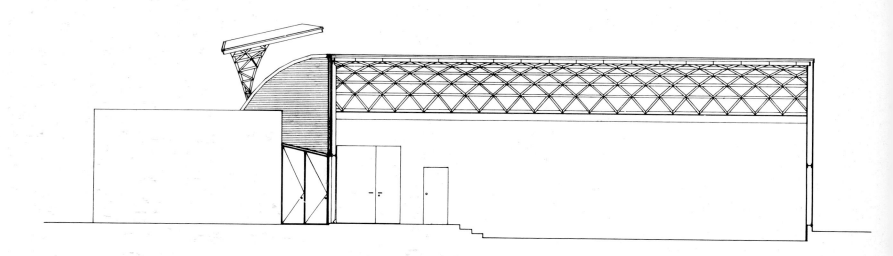

FROM ABOVE: Site plan; elevation; section

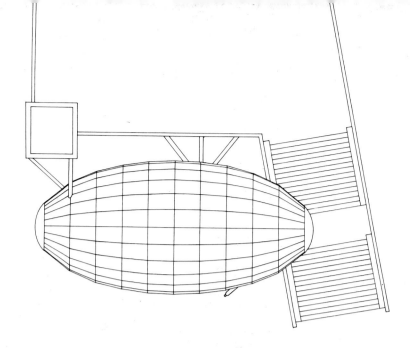

EGG OF WINDS
OKAWABATA RIVER CITY 21 TOWN GATE B

Tokyo, 1991

This rotating oval 'egg' 16 metres long and eight metres wide, floats four metres above ground on top of the entrance to a car park belonging the Okawabata River City 21 residential complex. Encased in 188 panels, 60 of which are perforated aluminium, it looks like a UFO when it reflects dim silver during the day. In the evening dusk as people come home from work, the in-built projection unit and lighting system start to operate, and silently transform the 'Egg of Winds' into a visual display unit.

Five liquid crystal projectors implanted in the egg transmit pictures on to two rear screens and on to the face of the perforated panels. The projected picture is computer controlled, involving three kinds of lighting equipment and combining five image sources.

The projectors which form the lighting source enable the Egg of Winds to present information and images which display a new kind of advertising space; where video artists may exhibit their work or where information for residents can be aired.

ABOVE: Part plan; BELOW: Elevation

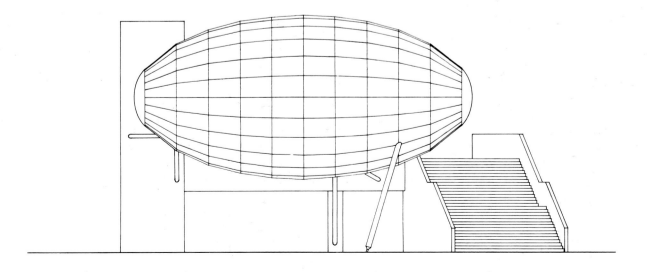

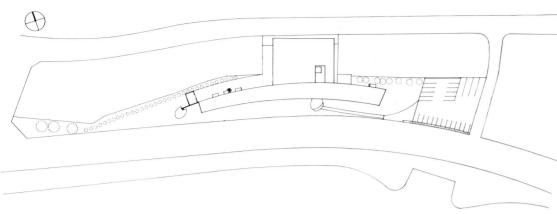

SHIMOSUWA MUNICIPAL MUSEUM

Nagano, 1992

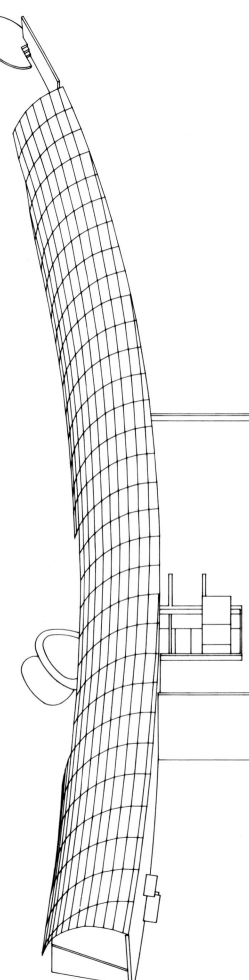

To commemorate the centennial of Shimosuwa, a city in the centre of the Nagano Prefecture, this is a reconstruction of the municipal museum on the shores of Lake Suwa. The design was selected in a competition held in June 1990. The new museum had to accommodate two permanent collections: materials and artefacts on the history and natural environment of Lake Suwa, and a collection from the life of the famous local poet Akahiko Shimagi. There are two volumes; the permanent exhibits are housed on the lakeside in a linear formation, with the north storage room on the mountain side. The walls, which stand along the curve of the site are covered with steel frames set every three

metres, drawing the structure in an arc toward the lake. A three-dimensional membrane emerges together with other arcs, in elevation and section, to cover this space.

The single most distinctive element is the aluminium panel covering the front of the building, giving it the appearance of an upside-down ship floating on the Suwa Lake. This curved surface resembles the hull of the ship cutting through the water's surface. This covering is particularly welcome in the cold climate and provides a double layer of waterproofing. As with the Yatsushiro Municipal Museum and The Tower of Winds, open-jointed panels are directly attached to the steel frame as

a part of the structural configuration.

Interior lighting fixtures and air-conditioning equipment are concealed in recesses in the ceilings and walls. Floor heating is provided by a supply of hot spring water which enhances the controlled nature of the environment.

The scenery of the lake is projected onto a glass screen, and is reflected by a thin layer of water in the courtyard, creating a rippling illusion of the exterior. The environment is therefore integrated with the building which as a whole becomes a flowing space.

LEFT: Axonometric; ABOVE: site plan

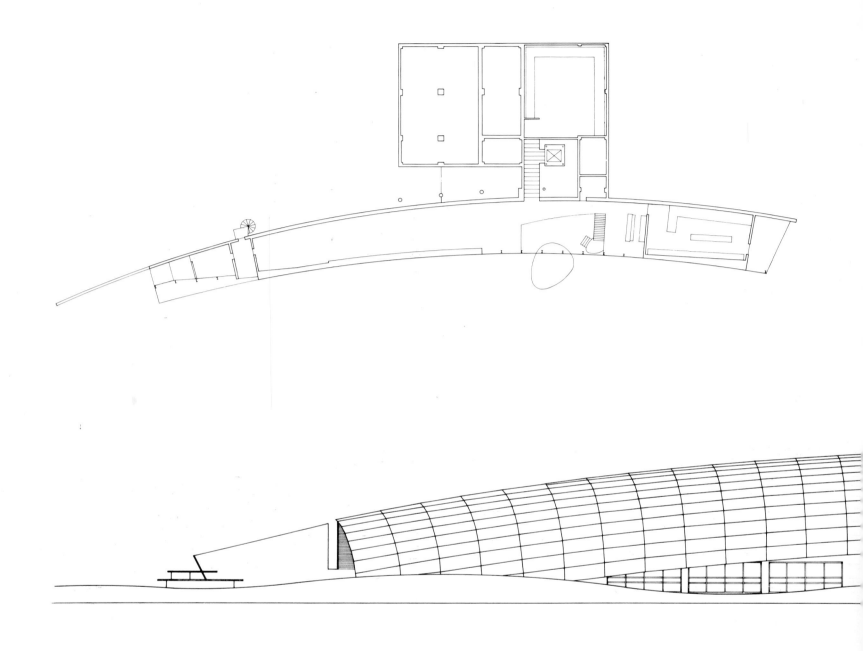

ABOVE, FROM L TO R: Floor plans for first and ground floors; CENTRE: Elevation

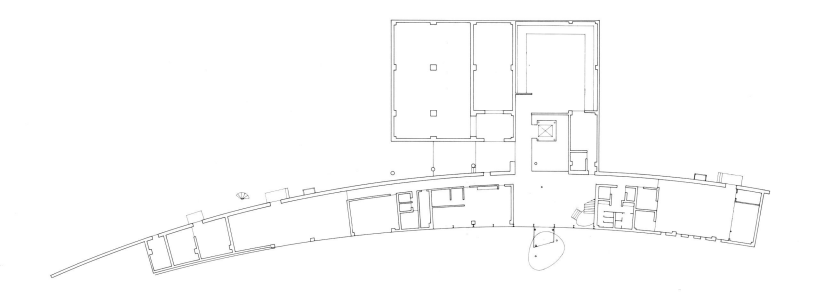

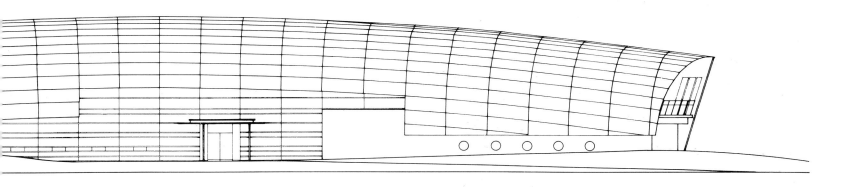

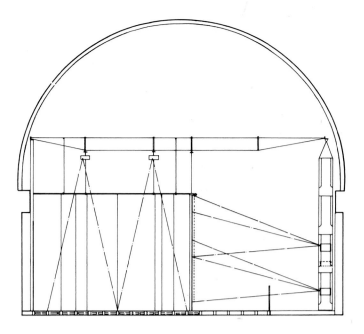

VISIONS OF JAPAN

London, 1991

This was an exhibition held at the Victoria and Albert Museum in London in 1991 which attempted to visualise in the form of clouds or mist the information particles emitted by various media in the city air.

It was an opportunity to replace the air of a classical Victorian space with beautiful and translucent noise, and to create 'visions' of Japan using a life-size liquid crystal glass facade, walls, floor and floating media output which directed visitors.

A waved screen formed a media wall which could be electronically controlled in transparency – a permeating membrane of information. In its translucent state the light particles from the video projector were transmitted onto the screen while light gradually permeated the media wall and projected onto the reflection panel

opposite, or on to the surfaces of visitors' clothing. The images of Tokyo city were incessantly screened randomly in the manner of a multi-media display.

The floating floor could also be manipulated in terms of light – the images slowly flowed on the resinous surface as if on still water. When light from the fluorescent tube under the floor increased, the room suddenly became the sea of 'Planet Solaris' – a white, soft space where all substances seemed to melt and disappear.

Five media terminals floated on the water surface: Bombom, Hyoro, Pukupuku, Dandan, Guruguru. These were linked with 'Tokyo city', allowing people to communicate interactively.

Section

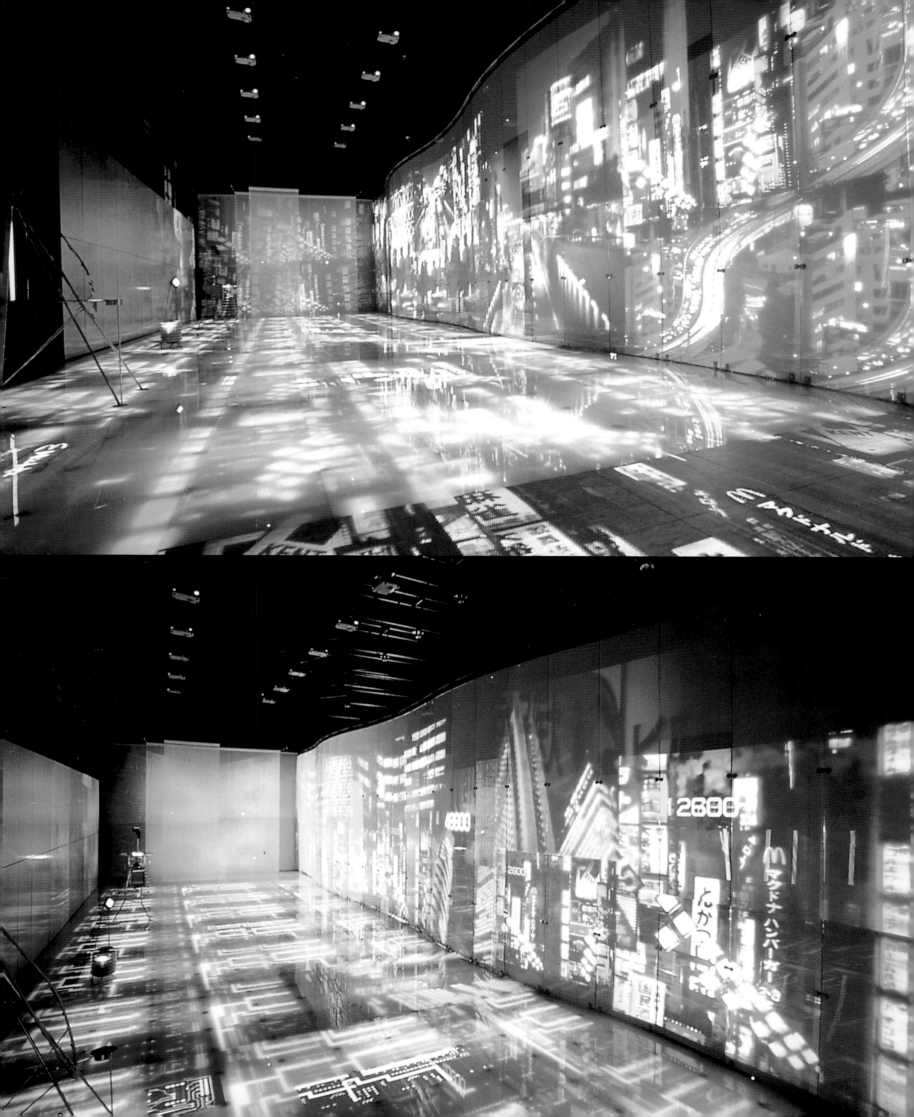

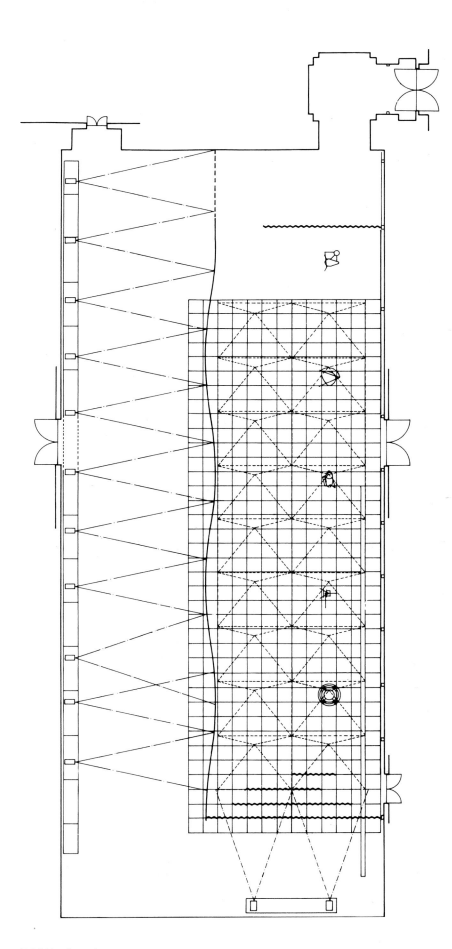

Exhibition floor plan

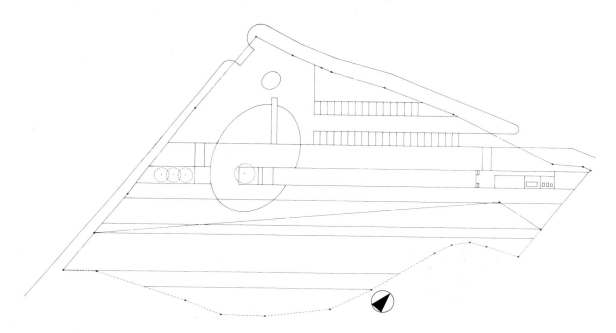

HOTEL P

Hokkaido, 1992

This hotel appears suddenly in the vast agricultural plane of Hokkaido. Although it is small in scale with only 26 guest rooms, fully equipped restaurant and meeting room, it has an authentic hotel atmosphere. The composition is simple: two floors of guest room compartments and a floor for the restaurant and lobby, thus providing high quality dining and accommodation facilities which are available to the local population. Despite the site conditions, the intention from the start was to create a kind of city hotel as an extension of urban space designed for individuals. In this sense, it represents an extremely abstract and artificial presence with respect to its environment.

Sentimentality is not the way to confront the challenge of the Hokkaido landscape. The site therefore consists of bold zones created by large stripes, each of which turns into green lawns, flower beds or artificial pave-

ment. All the guest rooms have a distant view of Mount Shari in the southeast. The oval shape of the public section, with parallel lines appearing in each of the rooms – articulating the interior and providing a sense of enclosure without defining a centre – results in the emergence of a highly transparent spatial quality.

The hotel forms a wall against nature almost as solid as concrete. The winding wall surrounds the inner space, as if protecting it from the grandeur of Hokkaido. This forms an urban air bubble which appears to float on the green meadow in summer, or on the snow plane in winter. The name 'Poluinya' is taken from a Russian word meaning a place in the midst of a white glacier where water remains without turning into ice.

ABOVE: Site plan; BELOW: South elevation

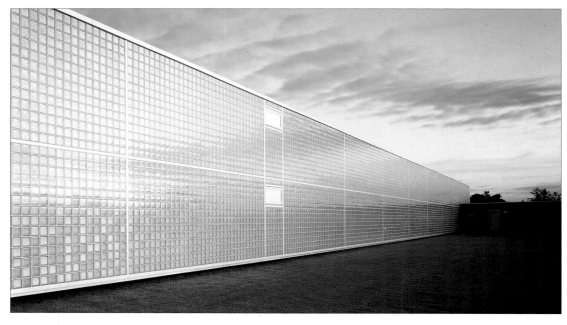

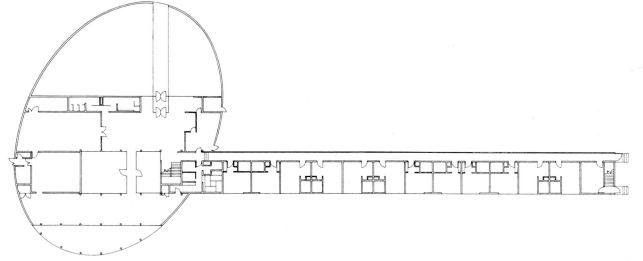

Ground floor plan

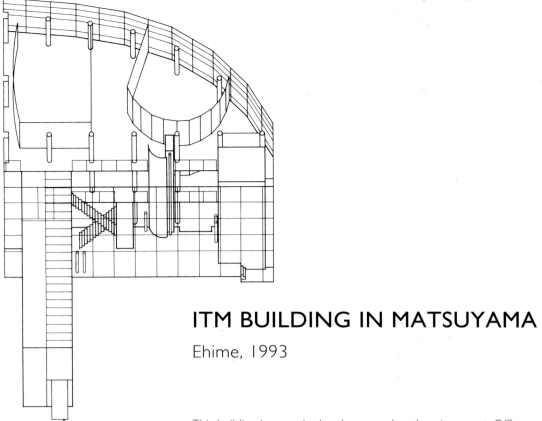

ITM BUILDING IN MATSUYAMA

Ehime, 1993

This building houses the head offices of the associated companies of the long-established confectioner Ichiroku. The site is in a residential district on the southern border of Matsuyama. The building, a dedicated office facility like the Nakameguro T building constructed in 1990, is classified in the Japanese Building Standards Act as an intermediate structure: between the completely fire resistant and the common wood building. It has a three-level 'void' space on the 1,500 square metre site containing stairways, small kitchen areas, toilets and other open-plan functions. This 'void' is a space animated by the presence of people and objects. It constitutes a new kind of 'communication location' where the people working can meet and chat in a relaxed environment. Offices are dispersed around the core, which itself houses the first-floor rectangular entrance hall, and the the second-floor break rooms.

Daylight is introduced from different directions in each individual functional area, and the result is a building filled with light. The three-level void space consists of a huge glass screen integrated with the structural columns. The glass is completely covered with a milky film that possesses a high interference characteristic to limit the influx of ultraviolet light and also softens the intensity of the afternoon sun. During the day, light for the offices comes through the multifaceted aluminium curtain wall shaped to fit the site.

Skylights are provided in the break rooms, allowing light to pass through the glass floor to the entrance hall beneath. The ITM is an open plan building – there are very few walls dividing the space. For this reason, indirect light provided in individual areas is dispersed, giving the interior of the building a homogeneous quality. Moreover, this light reflects off the aluminium, glass, white ceramic tile and other surfaces used, which break with the fixed conceptions of floor, wall, and ceiling. The subdued light emitted by these surfaces disturbs perceptions of direction: the interior of the building is suffused with a floating feeling as if it were utterly weightless.

Axonometric

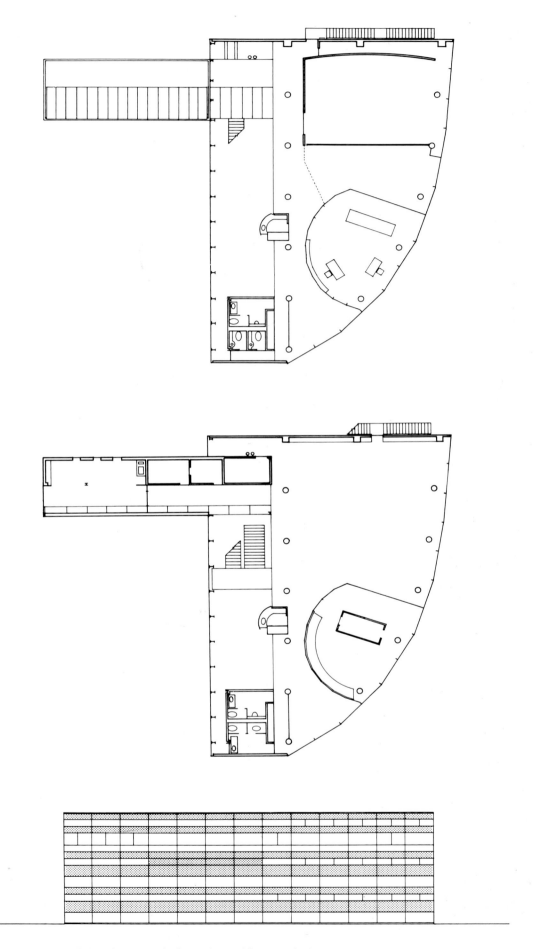

FROM ABOVE: Floor plans for first and ground floors; south elevation

TSUKUBA PARKING BUILDING

Ibaragi, 1994

Tsukuba Science City, with its broad, well-designed roads and large blocks devoted to single buildings, displays that unique sense of scale which identifies a new city produced as a planning project. The city is currently engaged in traffic planning that places primary emphasis on cars, and foresees a need to provide 10,000 parking spaces in multi-storey parking facilities. Tsukuba Parking Building, with capacity for 720 cars, is the second multi-storey parking building to be built in the centre of the Science City.

Given the simple and highly restrictive nature of such a building, attention was directed to three main issues: first, producing an efficient parking system; next, overcoming the structural problems posed by the system's formal requirements; and finally, how the building would participate visually in the city.

The parking system is unique in that it establishes up and down car ramps on the outside of the building, with direct access to each floor. Straight ramps running the length of the building were employed, instead of the traditional spiral access ramp, in order to efficiently accommodate parking spaces on the long narrow site. Since a continuous stream of cars entering the car park can be channelled off into floors with available space, congestion created by arriving and departing cars is alleviated. To fully equip the building for efficiency and comfort, there is a driver guidance system displaying textual information, and conveniently located auto-pay machines.

The rational approach of the building plan is reflected in its simple structure, a rigid frame with diagonal tie rod bracing. A 1.7-metre span between pillars in the parking areas promotes driver visibility, reducing the possibility of accidents. The exterior ramps are supported only by slender columns, and to maintain the lightweight impression of its steel frame, the building employs 'FR steel' – which does not need additional fireproofing protection.

The east-west facade is composed of aluminium louvres – a device which softens both the building's exterior appearance and the impact of the lights of parking cars on the neighbourhood. Employing two types of standard aluminium louvres, vertically and horizontally, the facade evokes the texture of a woven fabric, and contributes rhythm and delicacy to the 100-metre wall.

Multi-storey parking, because of its function and the stringency of its opening ratio, can easily become a cold, expressionless form of architecture that mars the urban landscape. In this building the dynamic form of the exterior ramps and the lightness of the louvred facade add to the townscape of the new city, and set a precedent for other parking buildings to be constructed here.

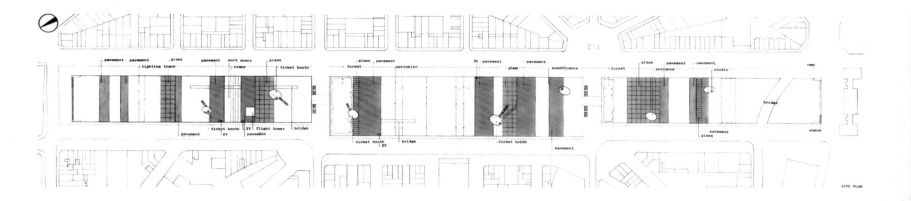

ANTWERP REJUVENATION PROJECT

Antwerp, 1992

In May 1990 Antwerp held the international competition 'Stad aan de Stroom' proposing the revitalisation of the city. Antwerp is a very beautiful Belgian city which has grown over several centuries on the banks of the river Scheldt. It has become one of the most important centres for water-based transportation in the modern world. The project was designed to bring people back to the waterfront district which they had previously abandoned with the move of harbour activities to the northern part of the city.

The area around the reclaimed dock in the Old South area of the city has the potential to become an excellent cultural district. A park was designed to include cultural facilities that would stimulate growth. First the dock was dug out to its original measurements 800 by 800 by 13 metres, and a garden on the ground, at depths varying from four to eight metres, was created

using bamboo, other plants, sand and artificial materials. Above this, the architectural functions are to be supported on a plane surface made by a flat bar form bridge, designed to suggest the water surface that once stretched across the dock here. Visitors pass through the interiors by way of tubes or bridges; they can also move under the 'bar coded' surface on the ground. This arrangement allows them to enjoy the sequence of super-impositions of the upper and lower spaces, and the variation in density of the activities within them.

The New South plan for the area next to this dock was a separate commission after the competition. The New South district is linked to the southern edge of the city, and the green site consists of more than 30 hectares within the junction of a freeway. An interface area, commercial spaces, offices,

residential and other facilities are planned for the district in order to bring new vitality to the city. Just like the South Dock, here too a green park will be provided and a linear volume placed above. In the garden, there is a pathway for pedestrians and bicycles, along which are located a library, meeting place and other facilities for the residents of the area. This stimulates interaction between the linear volume and the garden and generates human scale.

Several architects participated in the residential project, and thus only certain features of the residences were specified in advance. In terms of residential planning, the intention was to create continuous forms for each strip that would be linear and parallel.

New South area, general urban plan

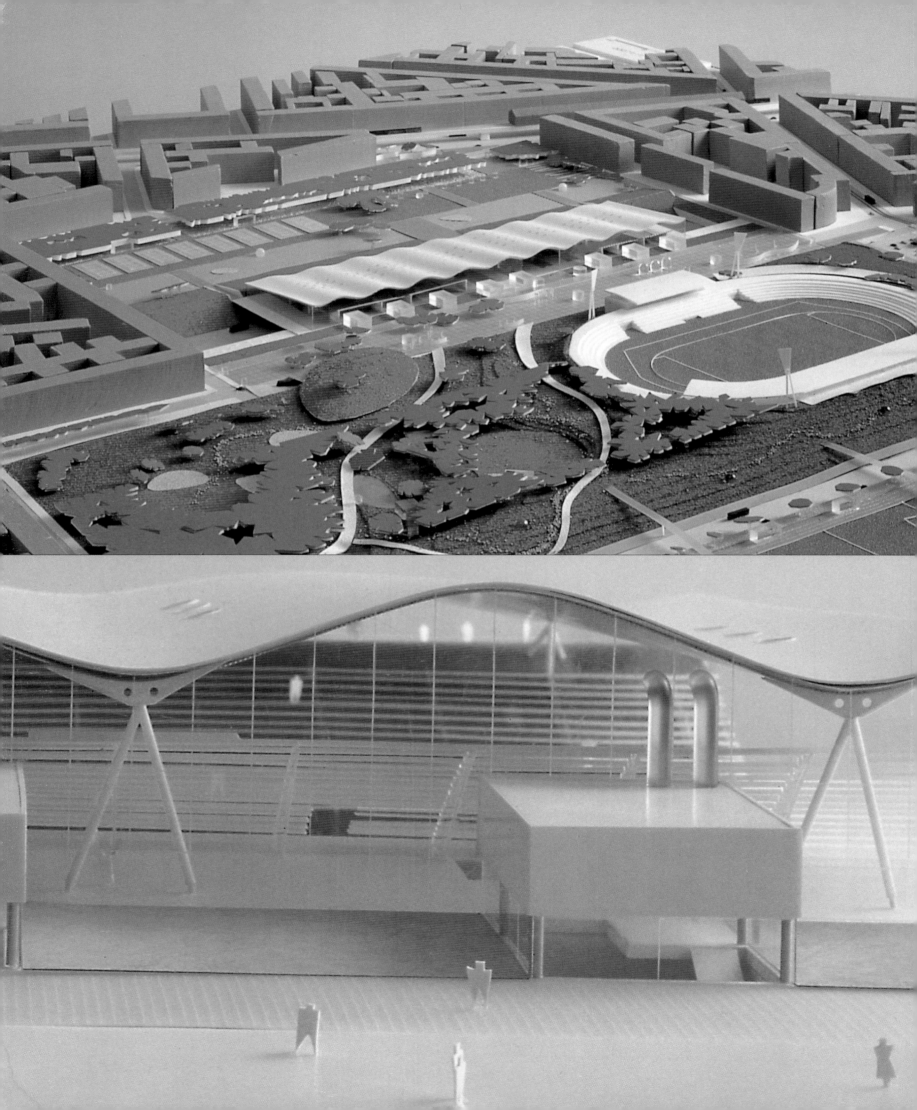

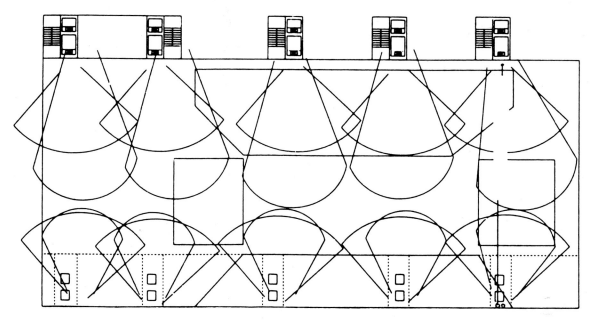

OLYMPIAD 2000 SPORTS HALLS

Berlin, 1992

The Olympiad 2000 project will see the city of Berlin greeting the twenty-first century from a new perspective. A system was proposed which provides two types of networks for the entire site; to create a natural environment synthesised with technology.

The site is divided into nine separate strips, enabling people and cars to flow through the gradual change in the landscape. The urban context and existing sports facilities determine the strip direction of north-south: creating a change in landscape, alternating levels and materials in response to functions. Together they express clarity, rationality and functionality.

Mass transportation is planned instead of private vehicles – the main approach to the site is directed towards the U-Bahn and S-Bahn stations. Planned facilities include boxing and judo halls (8,100 and 6,000 capacity respectively), and a main sports arena.

The main body of the Olympic hall is set into the earth. The spectator stand is composed of a simple steel structure, supported by a reinforced concrete box which forms the functional part of the stadium. Aluminium boxes along the west facade conceal the air-conditioning equipment, and the 'wavy shell' of the roof helps to conceal the three volumes beneath it, incorporating them into the landscape of the area as

a whole. Lighting across the site is used to create a space-like atmosphere, where pale blue and white lights set three metres high create a starry pattern along the ground.

The intention was to create a flexible building not designated for the Olympiad alone. After the games, certain elements will be removed: a proportion of the spectator seating – restoring the appearance of the valley and still providing a 3,000 capacity facility for public use. VIP rooms will be converted for public meetings and local sports associations.

ABOVE: Functional study; BELOW: Ventilation study

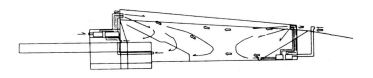

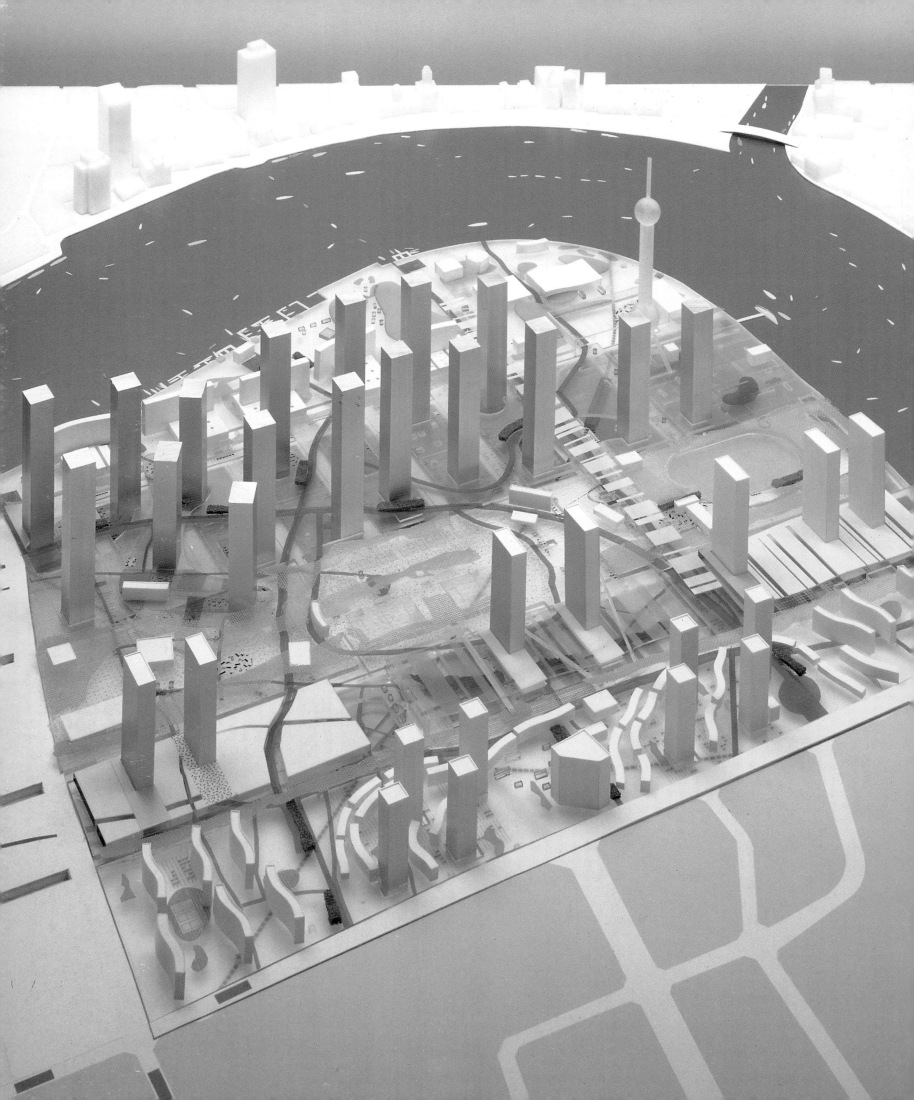

PLANNING AND URBAN DESIGN FOR SHANGHAI LUIJIAZUI CENTRAL AREA

Shanghai, 1992

A vast number of bicycles jostles through the streets beneath a skyline of high-rise office buildings and hotels. This is an everyday scene in Shanghai, a city which is now confronting major deficiencies in its basic infrastructure. Roads, bridges, and subways are affected as well as water supply and sewage disposal; the principle cause being excessive population density. Currently, the government of China is implementing a massive redevelopment plan for the district of Pudon on the opposite bank of the 500-metre wide Huang Pu river across from the old district, with the intention of making this area the economic centre of East Asia in the twenty-first century.

Located in the Pudon area, Luijiazui covers approximately 1.7 square kilometres. Designated a business district, it contains structures with a total floor area of almost four million square metres, including hotels, a conference centre, leisure, commercial, residential and cultural facilities, with the main focus on financial and trading company offices.

Bursting with the friendly energy generated in the atmosphere of confusion unique to the city of Shanghai, benefitting also from proximity to nature, history and technology, the goal here is a new city image.

The skeleton of the city is defined by the infrastructure of the subway at the lowest underground level, and the road system above. In addition, restoration was planned for the canal or creek network, which formerly served as the means of transportation for goods and the basis of traffic. A park formation was developed in which city trolley buses, bicycles and pedestrians moving on the ground can interact freely. Commercial, business, sports, residential, and other structures are arranged horizontally in 'bar code' formation. Lines of traffic are driven through the creek network destroying this parallel order. Although it may appear very complex, the initially opaque city structure is here extracted and clarified as a layered system. It is the diversity of people's activities generated precisely by the mutual relations between these layers that creates a new kind of co-ordination for the city. This is a context that accommodates all the dualistic oppositions of natural/artificial, order/disorder and rational/irrational. Adding this new stream to the special energy of Shanghai shapes a new high-density intelligent city with a form that now emerges into, and recedes from view.

Site plan

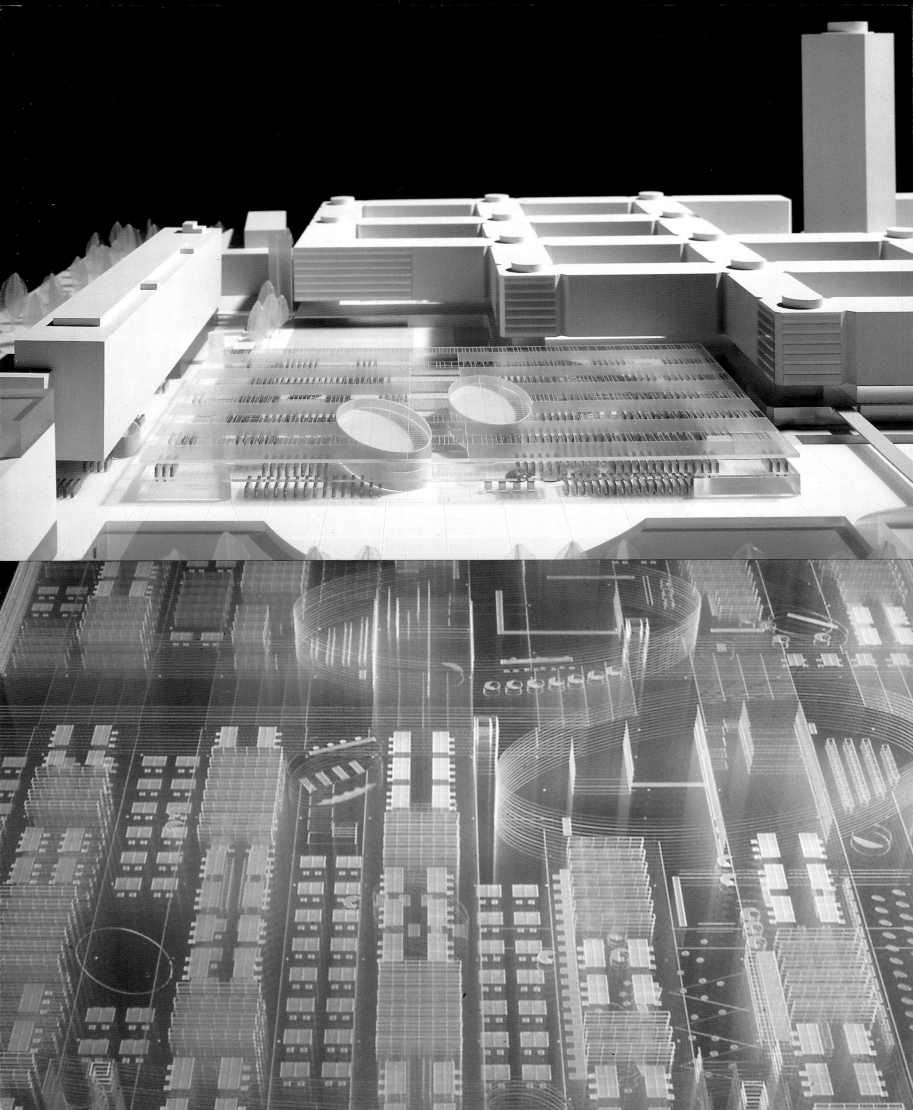

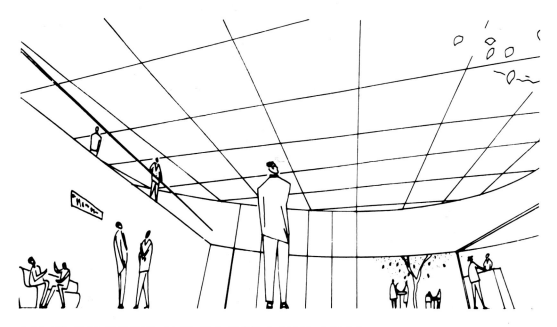

UNIVERSITY OF PARIS LIBRARY

Paris, 1992

The Jussieu competition, for which this project was an entry, had two basic goals: to design an entire campus for the Paris Universities and to produce a comprehensive library as a new central university location. The library was to be a combination of the two separate libraries for humanities and sciences, the latter of which in itself was a collection of eight small specialist libraries. An intricately interrelated complex, the basic character of this project was given by the indeterminacy of the plan itself. Strictly speaking it cannot be comprehended within either urban planning nor single architectural structure paradigms.

The site is near Notre Dame along the Seine: the Institut de Monde Arabe designed by Jean Nouvel stands in one corner of the campus. On a square site of approximately 500 metres, there already stands a vast facility with a total of 300,000 square metres of floor space built on an extremely rigorous grid system. This forms a kind of discrete city:

the strong parallel relationship to the Seine helps to restore and reinforce the urban scale of elements such as roads and campus buildings. However, like random distribution of plants in neighbouring gardens, people ramble through this space – it seemed that somewhere was required so people could gather in a relaxed atmosphere; a place with a pleasant vortex quality.

The image and basic functions of the library were to cater for the massive stock of books. The main activity specifies the architectural programme itself: processing, arranging and classifying books. The virtual space of a vast and transparent information matrix is created here. A physical space indispensable to the life of the campus, the library is also a source of communication for people on campus. The approach was to find a method of incorporating these conditions and phenomena into a physical body.

The essential task of introducing natural light was achieved not by taking in light from

conventional side openings, but from the roof surfaces instead. In this way the first and second levels are filled with a uniform light, creating space of a much better quality than ordinary interiors. The paralleled uniformity of the information area is manifested in the louvre form of the levels: skylights, the second floor, and the arrangements of bookshelves and furniture. The entrance hall is patterned in the same way as the surrounding green areas, and various booths are incorporated like follies within a garden so that people can wander among them. The curved enclosure of the campus plaza follows the wall of the library's reading rooms – superimposing geometrical forms in this way simultaneously connects and exchanges the functions of architecture and campus. An architectural, urban and visual body, this project is also a sensory phenomenon.

Perspective

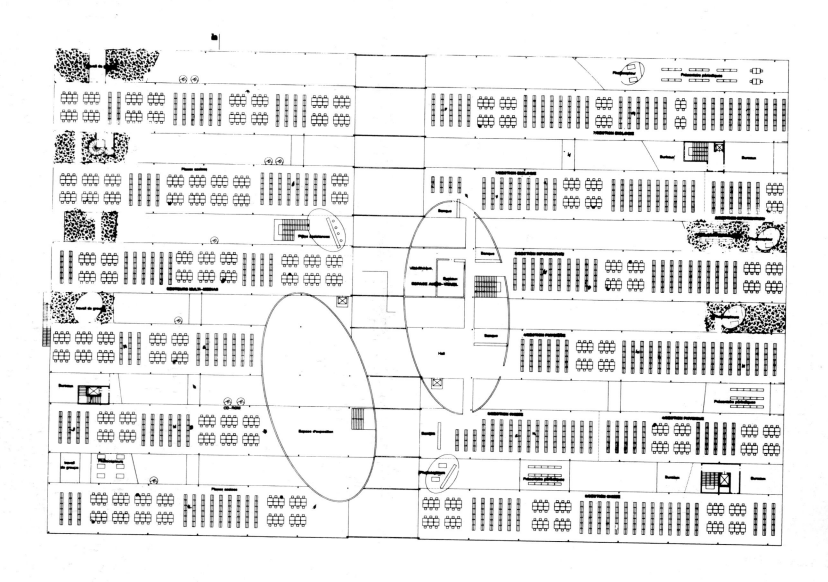

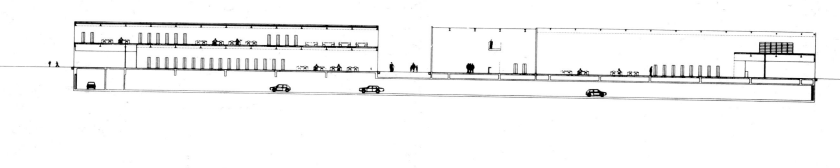

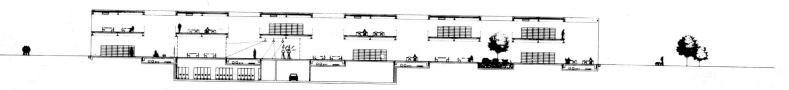

FROM ABOVE: Floor plan; sections

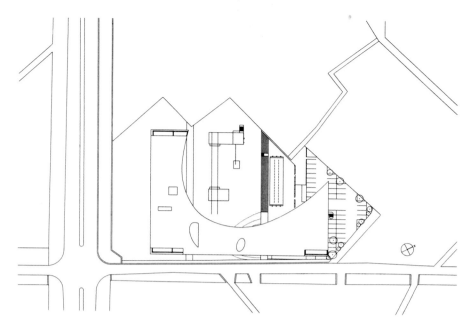

YATSUSHIRO FIRE STATION

Kumamoto, 1995

This fire station consists of a complex that comprises the Yatsushiro Regional Fire Service Headquarters, which has control over seven fire stations in the region, and the Yatsushiro Fire Station – a base for both fire fighting and emergency services in the centre of the city. Criteria for this project specified the most efficient and rational arrangement for the various fire station functions. Another intention was to create a very open, 'city park' space that was suited to the neighbouring environment: mostly residential with a local government centre. These requirements were processed in parallel, which made it possible to coordinate decisions on the numerous plans.

The volume containing offices, personnel sleeping quarters and other internal functions is elevated to a height of six metres above ground, and the training field area limited by a curved boundary. The internal space is thus an accumulation of sub-divided sections, the positions of which are determined from the priority of the function of each in relation to the emergency vehicle garage on the first floor.

The realisation of the project depended upon achieving ideal forms for two very different environments: the 'park' and an optimally functional fire station. The result is a unique combination of the two.

Site plan

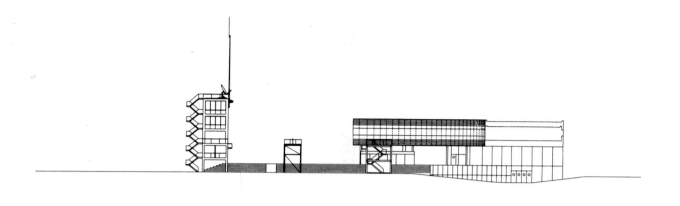

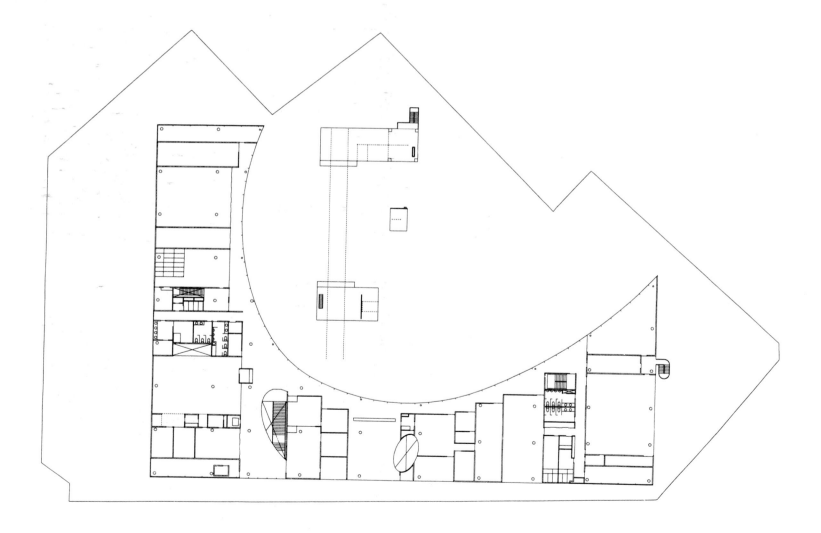

FROM ABOVE: Elevation; upper floor plan

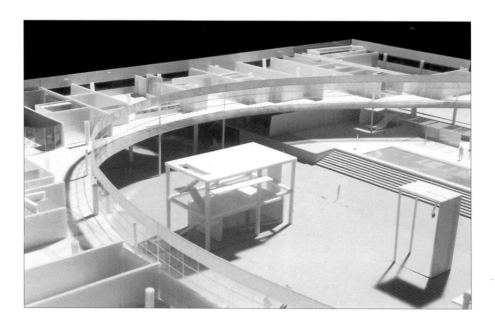

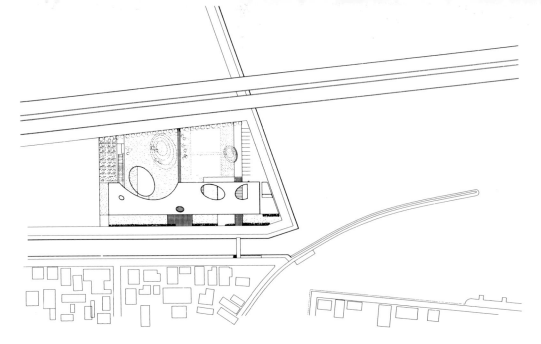

OLD PEOPLE'S HOME IN YATSUSHIRO

Kumamoto, 1994

This project is situated on a new area of land reclaimed from the sea beside the fishing harbour in Hinagu, and accommodates fifty senior citizens in a small community on the coast of the Shiranui Sea. The plan involved creating an improved facility on a new site, adhering to the organisational model of the hospital, yet overcoming the 'architecture of confinement' that this usually tends to produce.

The building is 100 metres in length, along which a corridor runs against a single line of rooms; designed to maximise sunlight requirements. On the other side of the corridor, the dining room, bathrooms, meeting rooms and other common facilities are positioned according to acceptable walking distances and frequency of use. The building is set back towards the mountains to reduce traffic noise from a major new road, and faces directly onto the existing neighbourhood.

The flat roof utilises metal decking with a 100 millimetre flange, used as a continuous series of shallow secondary beams. Only primary beams were necessary across the breadth of the roof, and these are hidden within the joints between the decking panels. This emphasises the flat, lightweight form of the roof.

The elements below the roof: colour, materials and spaces, are distributed seemingly without design, to such an extent that they appear marked by a sense of fracture. Features such as the courtyard and the rooftop garden are extremely artificial, almost like stage props generating distinct views. The spaces of the building are loosely arranged to achieve a soft blending of territories.

This project operates as both a medical and an educational facility, and can be thought of as a large residence for a family of fifty, or as a long-term residential hotel with fifty rooms. One principal design intention was to produce a simple solution for a building type whose typical architectural programme often tends to be very complex. The resulting layout seems akin to automatic writing, and has appeared in several projects since the competition proposal for the Japanese Maison de la Culture in Paris.

This building illustrates the striking of a balance with efficiency: to give the closed configuration of a nursing home the loosest possible arrangement – one with the openness of a public place. The building has a relaxed atmosphere that will tempt even non-residents to casually drop in as they pass. The meeting rooms open out on to a broad expanse of greenery which promotes a wide range of activities such as croquet matches, the spring movie festival, summer fireworks displays, the autumn harvest festival, and kite flying in the winter.

A facility that for management purposes tends to be typically closed to the outside world, should ideally be open to the town and operate as a gathering place within it.

Site plan

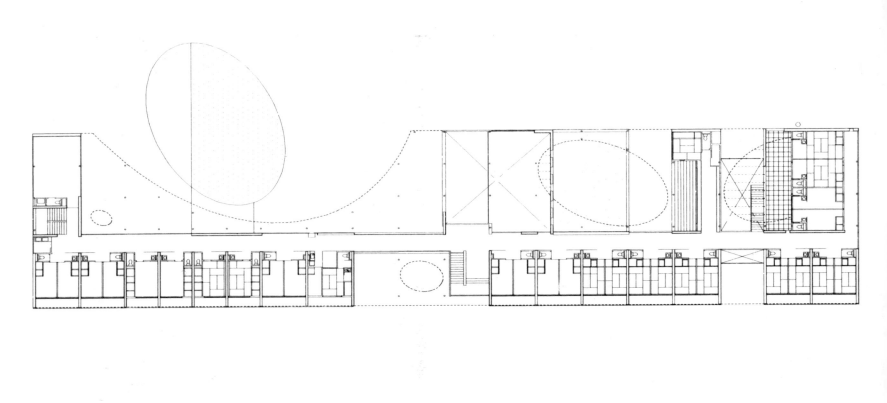

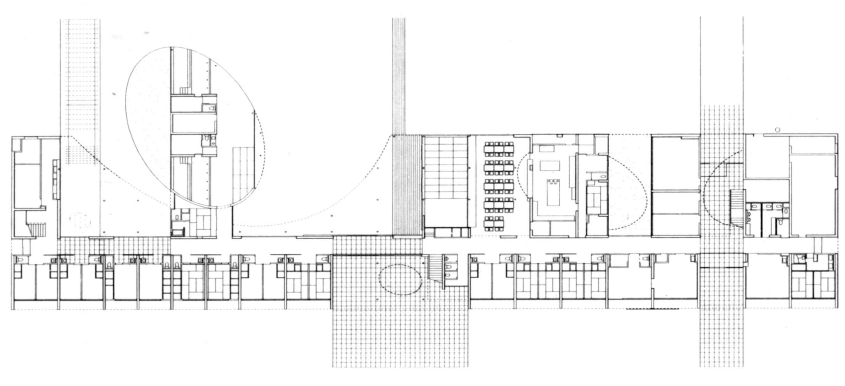

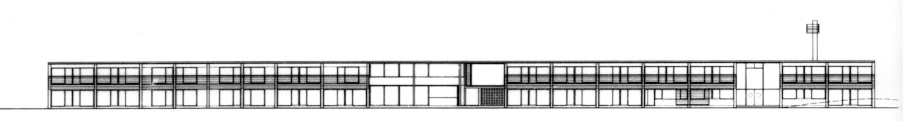

OPPOSITE, FROM ABOVE: Floor plans for first and ground floors; elevation

Tower of Winds

BIOGRAPHY

1941 Born in Seoul
1965 Graduated from Department of Architecture, Tokyo University
1965-9 Worked for Kiyonori Kikutake Architect and Associates
1971 Established Urban Robot (URBOT) in Tokyo
1979 Changed company name to Toyo Ito & Associates, Architects

Awards and Prizes

1979 First prize, restricted competition for Japan Airlines Ticket Counter
1984 Japan Architects Association Award for House in Kasama
1986 Architectural Institute of Japan Award for Silver Hut
First prize, restricted competition for the Tower of Winds
1987 Japan Interior Designers Association Award for Nomad Restaurant and other works
1988 First prize, restricted competition for the Reconstruction Project for the Opera House in Frankfurt
First prize, restricted competition for the 89 ARTEC Nagoya Biennale Pavilion
1990 Togo Murano Award for Guest House for Sapporo Breweries
1992 Mainichi Art Award for Yatsushiro Municipal Museum
1993 BCS Award for Yatsushiro Municipal Museum
First prize, restricted competition for Nagaoka Municipal Cultural and Art Hall
First prize, restricted competition for Taishacho Municipal Cultural Hall

Exhibitions

1978 'The New Wave of Japanese Architecture', New York
'Post Metabolism', Architectural Association, London
1981 'The House as an Image', Louisiana Museum, USA and Copenhagen
'Biennale de Paris', Paris
1984 'Japan Air', Rotterdam
1985 'TOKYO in Tokyo' with Kohei Sugiura at Laforet Museum, Tokyo
1986 'Architecture in the City of Winds', one man exhibition, Gallery Ma, Tokyo
'Tokyo: Form and Spirit', Walker Art Centre, Minneapolis
'Toyo Ito Architecture per una Citta Argentata', Fiesole
'Anemorphosis: Transformations by Wind', Tokyo
1987 'Architecture International Series 1987', Sydney and Melbourne
1989 'The Case Study Houses', MOCA 90, Los Angeles
'Institut Francais d'Architecture', Paris
'Salon International de l'Architecture', Paris
'Transfiguration – Europalia 89', Brussels
1990 'IN ARCH', Rome
1991 'Institut Francais d'Architecture', Paris
'Visions of Japan', Victoria and Albert Museum, London
1992 'Yokohama Urban Ring', Spril Hall, Tokyo
'Abitale Italia – Good Living Show in Harumi', Tokyo
'Toyo Ito', Tooricho Gallery, Tokyo
1993 'Architecture of the Year 93', Met Hall, Tokyo
'Electronic Surface, Liquid Structure', O Museum, Tokyo

Conferences and Visiting Lecturer

1978 Tokyo Zoukei University
1979 Chiba University
1981-3 Tokyo Institute of Technology
1982 P3 Conference, Charlottesville, Virginia
1983 Tokyo University
1984 Tokyo Denki University
Pratt Institute, New York
Japan Air, Rotterdam
1984-7 Wasada University
1985 Academie van Beeldende, Kunsten, Rotterdam
1988 Japan Women's University
1988-9 Tokyo University
1989 Fukuoka International Architects' Conference '89, Fukuoka
Nagoya Design Conference, Aichi Prefecture
1990 Tohoku University
Nagoya University
1991 Columbia University, New York
1993 Symposium 'Electronic Surface, Liquid Structure', O Museum, Tokyo
'A Garden of Microchips' lecture, Kenchiku Kaikan, Tokyo

Publications

1981 Translation of *The Mathematics of The Ideal Villa and Other Essays* by Colin Rowe
1986 'Toyo Ito – Kaze no Henyotai (Transfiguration of Winds)', Kajima Insititute Publishing
1988 *Toyo Ito*, Shinkenchiku-sha
1989 'Kaze no Henyotai – Transfiguration of Winds', Seidosha
1991 *Toyo Ito Architecture Fluctuante*, IFA, France
Toyo Ito, Architecture monograph by Sophie Roulet and Sophie Soulié, Editions du Moniteur
1992 *Architecture in a Simulated City*, INAX
'Yatsushiro Municipal Museum', photographed by Mitsumasa Fujitsuka, TOTO
1993 *JA library 2: Toyo Ito*, Shinkenchiku-sha

CHRONOLOGY OF WORKS 1971-95

House in Kasama

1971
Aluminum House
Location: Tsujido, Kanagawa
Site area: 379.18 m²
Building area: 84.24 m²
Total floor area: 110.16 m²
Programme: house
Number of storeys: 2

1974
Cottage in Sengataki
Location: Nagano
Site area: 995.83 m²
Building area: 58.59 m²
Total floor area: 62.85 m²
Programme: house
Number of storeys: 2

1975
Black Recurrence
Location: Setagaya, Tokyo
Site area: 85.95 m²
Building area: 42.53 m²
Total floor area: 80.20 m²
Programme: house
Number of storeys: 2

1976
White U
Location: Nakano, Tokyo
Site area: 367.61 m²
Building area: 150.97 m²
Total floor area: 148.25 m²
Programme: house
Number of storeys: 1

1976
House in Kamiwada
Location: Okazaki, Aichi
Site area: 197.98 m²
Building area: 90.58 m²
Total floor area: 90.58 m²
Programme: house
Number of storeys: 1

1977
Hotel D
Location: Sugadaira, Nagano
Site area: 5,242 m²
Building area: 1,152.48 m²
Total floor area: 2,437.24 m²
Programme: hotel
Number of storeys: 2

1978
PMT Building
Location: Nagoya, Aichi
Site area: 726.88 m²
Building area: 428.20 m²
Total floor area: 920.92 m²
Programme: offices
Number of storeys: 4

1979
PMT Building
Location: Fukuoka-shi, Fukuoka
Site area: 897.18 m²
Building area: 457.32 m²
Total floor area: 895.27 m²
Programme: offices
Number of storeys: 2

1979
PMT Factory
Location: Neyagawa-shi, Osaka
Site area: 2,120.06 m²
Building area: 1,098 m²
Total floor area: 2,236.18 m²
Programme: factory
Number of storeys: 2

1979
House in Koganei
Location: Koganei-shi, Tokyo
Site area: 146.76 m²
Building area: 50.05 m²
Total floor area: 93.91 m²
Programme: house
Number of storeys: 2

1979
House in Chuorinkan
Location: Yamato, Nara
Site area: 127.76 m²
Building area: 73.61 m²
Total floor area: 122.40 m²
Programme: house
Number of storeys: 2

1981
House in Kasama
Location: Ibaragi
Site area: 865.48 m²
Building area: 155.24 m²
Total floor area: 289.91 m²
Programme: house
Number of storeys: 2

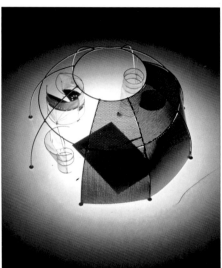

FROM ABOVE: House in Hanakoganei; Pao I
Exhibition Project for Pao: a Dwelling for Tokyo
Nomad Women; Furniture for Tokyo Nomad Women

1982
House in Umegaoka
Location: Setagaya-ku, Tokyo
Site area: 137.73 m²
Building area: 60.30 m²
Total floor area: 117.88 m²
Programme: house
Number of storeys: 2

1983
House in Hanakoganei
Location: Kodaira-shi, Tokyo
Site area: 242.30 m²
Building area: 77 m²
Total floor area:152.20 m²
Programme: house
Number of storeys: 2

1983
House in Denenchofu
Location: Ota-ku, Tokyo
Site area: 161.10 m²
Building area: 69.11 m²
Total floor area: 134.96 m²
Programme: house
Number of storeys: 2

1984
Silver Hut
Location: Nakano-ku, Tokyo
Site area: 403.46 m²
Building area: 119.99 m²
Total floor area:138.81 m²
Programme: house
Number of storeys: 2

1985
Pao I Exhibition Project for Pao: a Dwelling
for Tokyo Nomad Women
Location: Seibu Department Store, Tokyo
Programme: Furniture

1985
Project for the Sports Complex in Owani
Location: Minami-Tugaru-gun, Aomori
Prefecture
Programme: sports complex
Number of storeys: 1

1986
House in Magomezawa
Location: Funabashi-shi, Chiba
Site area: 100 m²
Building area: 49.65 m²
Total floor area: 81.18 m²
Programme: house
Number of storeys: 2

1986
Furniture for Tokyo Nomad Women

1986
Honda Automobile Showroom
Location: Setagaya-ku, Tokyo
Site area: 238.84 m²
Building area: 180.53 m²
Total floor area: 393.03 m²
Programme: showroom
Number of storeys: 3

1986
Nomad Restaurant
Location: Minato-ku, Tokyo
Site area: 332.80 m²
Building area: 272.46 m²
Total floor area: 428.93 m²
Programme: restaurant
Number of storeys: 3

1986
Tower of Winds
Location: Yokohama-shi, Kanagawa
Site area: 43.45 m²
Programme: reconstruction of an
obsolete tower
Height: 21.10 m

1986
Project for House in Saijo
Location: Hiroshima
Site area: 1,848.05 m²
Building area: 200.17 m²
Total floor area: 242.17 m²
Programme: house
Number of storeys: 2

1986
Project for Fujisawa Municipal Cultural
Complex
Location: Kanagawa
Site area: 7,970.30 m²
Building area: 4,015.30 m²
Total floor area: 12,280 m²
Programme: cultural complex
Number of storeys: 3

1987
M Building in Kanda
Location: Chiyoda-ku, Tokyo
Site area: 142.43 m²
Building area: 128.06 m²
Total floor area: 671.26 m²
Programme: offices
Number of storeys: 6

1987
Project for Noh Theatre
Programme: theatre with 3,000 seats

FROM ABOVE: Project for House in Saijo; M Building in Kanda; lighting design for the Frankfurt Opera House; Pastina Restaurant

1987
MAC Project
Location: Machida, Tokyo
Site area: 5,800 m²
Building area: 4,700 m²
Total floor area: 43,700 m²
Programme: commercial complex
Number of storeys: 9

1988
House in Takagicho
Location: Minato-ku, Tokyo
Site area: 202.80 m²
Building area: 120.94 m²
Total floor area: 324.20 m²
Programme: house
Number of storeys: 3

1988
Roof Garden Project
Location: Tokyo

1988
Opera House
Location: Frankfurt, Germany
Programme: ceiling of the main auditorium

1988
Furniture in Italy

1989
Guest House for Sapporo Breweries
Location: Eniwa-shi, Hokkaido
Site area: 318,368.90 m²
Building area: 1,196.50 m²
Total floor area: 1,138.70 m²
Programme: guest house
Number of storeys: 1

1989
Pastina Restaurant
Location: Setagaya-ku, Tokyo
Site area: 181.31 m²
Building area: 122.84 m²
Total floor area: 340.91 m²
Programme: restaurant
Number of storeys: 2

1989
Pao II Exhibition Project for Pao: a Dwelling for Tokyo Nomad Women
Location: Brussels, Belgium ('Transfiguration – Europalia' Exhibition)

1989
I Building in Asakusabashi
Location: Taito-ku, Tokyo
Site area: 127.23 m²
Building area: 97.46 m²
Total floor area: 676.10 m²

Programme: offices
Number of storeys: 9

1990
T Building in Nakameguro
Location: Meguro-ku, Tokyo
Site area: 584.05 m²
Building area: 401.57 m²
Total floor area: 1,443.77 m²
Programme: offices
Number of storeys: 3

1990
Project for Japanese Maison de la Culture
Location: Paris, France
Site area: 1,670 m²
Building area: 1,260 m²
Total floor area: 6,865 m²
Programme: municipal complex
Number of storeys: 6

1991
Visions of Japan
Location: Victoria and Albert Museum, London
Programme: exhibition

1991
Yatsushiro Municipal Museum
Location: Yatsushiro-shi, Kumamoto
Site area: 8,223.20 m²
Building area: 1,432.89 m²
Total floor area: 3,418.31 m²
Programme: museum
Number of storeys: 4

1991
Gallery U in Yugawara
Location: Kanagawa
Site area: 1,275.70 m²
Building area: 267.10 m²
Total floor area: 256.20 m²
Programme: gallery
Number of storeys: 2

1991
Okawabata River City 21 Town Gate B (Egg of Winds)
Location: Chuo-ku, Tokyo
Building area: 118.53 m²
Programme: main gate

1992
Shimosuwa Municipal Museum
Location: Shimosuwa-cho, Nagano
Site area: 5,275.55 m²
Building area: 1,369.99 m²
Total floor area: 1,982.78 m²
Programme: museum
Number of storeys: 2

1992
Hotel P
Location: Shari-gun, Hokkaido
Site area: 6,604.36 m²
Building area:982.93 m²
Total floor area: 1,417.8 m²
Programme: hotel
Number of storeys: 2

1992
Public Kindergarten in Eckenheim
Location: Frankfurt, Germany
Site area: 2,900 m²
Building area: 653 m²
Total floor area: 703 m²
Programme: kindergarten
Number of storeys: 1

1992
Planning and Urban Design for Shanghai
Luijiazui Central Area
Location: Shanghai
Site area: 170 hectares
Total floor area: 4,000,000 m²
Programme: planning and urban design
Height: 240 m

1992
Project for the Olympiad 2000 Sports Halls
Location: Berlin
Total floor area: 40,000 m²
Programme: sports hall
Number of storeys: 3

1992
Project for the University of Paris Library
Location: Paris
Site area: 126,433 m²
Building area: 14,755 m²
Total floor area: 19,710 m²
Programme: library
Number of storeys: 3

1992
Antwerp Rejuvenation Project
Location: Antwerp
Site area: 59 hectares
Building area: 238,390 m²
Programme: park, residences, cultural and
commercial institutions

1993
ITM Building in Matsuyama
Location: Matsuyama-shi, Ehime
Site area: 831.66 m²
Building area: 486.37 m²
Total floor area: 1,255.68 m²
Programme: office building

1993
Amusement Complex H
Location: Tama-shi, Tokyo
Site area: 6,400m²
Building area: 4,570 m²
Total floor area: 23,830 m²
Programme: commercial complex
Number of storeys: 7

1994
Tsukuba Parking Building
Location: Ibaragi Prefecture
Site area: 6,477 m²
Building area: 4,904 m²
Total floor area: 20,433 m²
Programme: car park
Number of storeys: 6

1994
Old People's Home in Yatsushiro
Location: Yatsushiro-shi, Kumamoto
Site area: 7,425 m²
Building area: 2,183 m²
Total floor area: 2,467 m²
Programme: old people's home
Number of storeys: 2

1995
Yatsushiro Fire Station (under construction)
Location: Yatsushiro-shi, Kumamoto
Site area: 8,390 m²
Building area: 3,329 m²
Total floor area: 5,392 m²
Programme: fire station
Number of storeys: 3

Japanese Airlines Counters
Fukuoka (2), Sendai, Kobe, Niigata, Chiba,
Nagasaki, Tokyo, Sapporo, Kanazawa, Nagoya,
Hiroshima, Matsuyama, Imperial Hotel in
Tokyo, Kyoto, Hong Kong (3), Madrid, Moscow,
Oakland, Vancouver, Frankfurt (2), Chicago,
Munich, Copenhagen, Seattle, Mexico City,
Brussels, London, Rio de Janeiro, Beijing,
Karachi, Athens, Dusseldorf, Kuala Lumpur,
Hamburg, Geneva, Honolulu, Atlanta, Bangkok,
Shanghai, Washington DC, Jakarta, San
Francisco, Manila, Sydney, Zurich, Los Angeles,
Seoul, Pusan, Singapore, New York, Paris

FROM ABOVE: Pao II; JAL Ticket Counter, New York

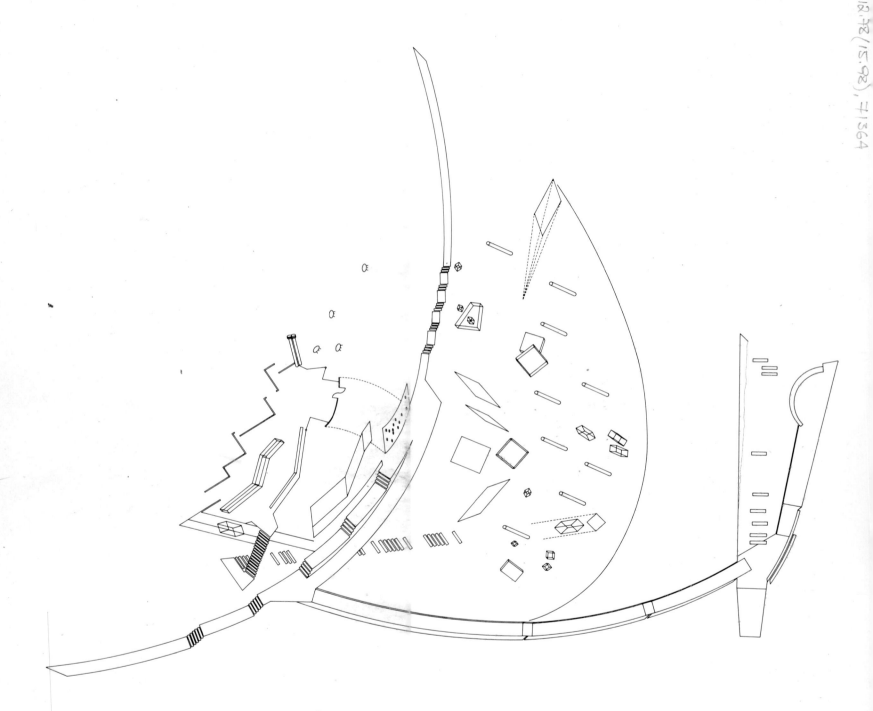

Yatsushiro Municipal Museum, exploded schematic interior